AMISHLAND

AMIS

HLAND

by

Kiehl and Christian Newswanger

HASTINGS HOUSE PUBLISHERS NEW YORK

TO

DR. CHRISTIAN H. NEUSWANGER
Formerly member of the faculty of Yale Medical School,
in gratitude for his help.

Contents

FOREWORD

I MADE my first drawing of Samuel Petersheim Stoltzfus, which is shown on page 11, in 1920. It was what might be termed a naturalistic portrait, in that it was a truthful imitation of the outward appearance of the subject. But it in no way satisfied the desire I then had to express the "inner spirit" of the Amish.

The present volume sums up my efforts and those of my son Christian, since that time, to interpret the Amish in a form that is visually related to their actual philosophy of life. What we have done here stems from our own experience while living among the Amish who are our friends and neighbors — people whose unique way of living demands from its interpreter a very special mode of expression.

We hope our drawings and the accompanying text express what we have come to believe is the essence of the Amish philosophy which manifests itself to the casual observer in a rigid religious discipline and "quaintness" in dress, manners and customs. We believe the "inner life" of the Amish has contributed an important if small element to the general picture of America.

It should be understood that the superficial characteristics of these people, which make them so different from their "worldly" neighbors, are nothing more than the outer evidences of their grim determination to preserve intact a culture which was already time-tested when they transplanted it from Switzerland and Germany to America more than two hundred years ago.

The Amish are essentially a farming people. They are one of the few groups that migrated to America because of unbearable religious persecution; in their case the persecution resulted from their absolute refusal to bear arms for any reason whatsoever (for Christ said, "Love thine enemies") — a principle which they have continued to adhere to up to the present day.

They have as nearly as possible retained the dress, customs, and more important, the religious beliefs and thought and the religious forms evolving from these latter, that have so long proved right for them.

The Amish use no modern machinery to make their farming easier or leave them time for idleness. They are first-rate farmers — have always practiced contour farming and the rotation of crops to maintain the fertility of the soil. In the face of keen competition from neighbors who use the latest techniques of mechanized farming, they continue to produce the highest possible yield from some of the most productive land in America, the fertility of which they have not only kept up but also increased for the benefit of their sons and sons' sons.

The original Amish settlers did not come to America to start a new life but to preserve the old way of living. The artist sees in this group of the Old Order Amish which today numbers some four thousand persons in Lancaster County, certain definite and pronounced types that are the outcome of generations of intermarriage. You find a somewhat similar type of facial structure among the Kings and Queens of Judaea on the Portail Royal of Chartres Cathedral — sculptures executed in the twelfth century.

The Bible, the family and the farm are the foundation on which the Amish build their lives. In order to get a deeper insight into these elements that go to make up the sum total of their living, I began to work with and for these people when I moved my studio into the heart of the Amish country a few miles due east of Lancaster in Pennsylvania. I helped them cultivate their fields, plant and harvest their crops, went to market with them, took part in their barn-raisings — and enjoyed their good food and good fellowship. Very gradually, little by little, I began to understand the way the Amish live, developed a profound respect for their religious discipline and took a real part in their communal activities. My spirit was touched by their gentleness.

The strenuous physical labor that Amish farm life entails was not the hardship, as far as I was concerned, that it might have been to another, since I had spent many years on my grandparents' farm as a child. When I went to live among the Amish I rediscovered the love of the land which must have been lying fallow in me all those years.

My grandparents had nine sons, of which my father was the eldest. Plenty of activities took place on the farm besides just hard work. I remember hunting and trapping along the River Hills, fishing in the Susquehanna, and driving grandmother, decked out in her black bonnet and Sunday gray, to the Mennonite Meeting at New Providence. There was the daily chore of taking milk to the creamery at the little hamlet known as the Buck, and the pleasant task of helping my young uncles wash their buggies at the Mine Holes, an abandoned quarry.

Nine boys in the family were a great convenience when it came to making up a baseball team or a band, and I well remember concerts at Unicorn and ball games of the Quarryville team, made up chiefly of my uncles, playing against Oxford. School entertainments at White Oak Bottom, which I attended with my

uncles, reminded me sharply that my roots were deep in Lancaster County soil. Here my ancestor, seven generations back, named, Christian Newswanger, had founded our homestead. Family records reveal that he died in the harvest field, of a sunstroke, at the age of forty-five, leaving a widow and seven children.

The text of this book, written by my son Christian, tells about the many little things, the daily happenings, which built up the sum total of our life among the Amish. Both my sons while we were living among these people in order that I might learn their ways and interpret their spiritual attitudes, were of course brought under the influence of the Amish way of life, although not as intimately as I was. As they grew old enough they went into the fields — to market, to butcherings and barn-raisings — and they learned by living in close contact with the Amish the strict and unyielding discipline under which their children live. These children are trained from their earliest years in farm work as well as in religion to become industrious, frugal and God-fearing. They are denied the elaborate toys the city neighbors give their youngsters; but when the time comes for an Amish boy to establish a family of his own, the father will help him by buying the farm for him. And then the heritage of the godly man and the good farmer passes on from father to son.

My son Christian is seven years older than his brother Peter, and because he was a growing active boy our Amish neighbors soon cast their eyes on him — but chiefly on his strong back — and so he joined in the farm work too. He chose to apprentice himself to me as an artist, and he found the slow, laborious pace of Amish life the beginning for him of the equally slow and laborious development of an art form.

Just as the Amish whose dress is always patterned after their old fashions, and whose habits and customs are changeless, had withdrawn from the main current of civilization to insure survival of their beliefs and way of living, so also we found we had to withdraw from the swift, competitive and precipitous stream of modern life, to make it possible for our art form to germinate in the only way it could — quietly and gradually.

My cousin, Dr. Christian Neuswanger, to whom this book is dedicated, and without whose help and patient forebearance it might never have been completed, was the son of Amish parents and was brought up in the strict Amish ways. He believes this boyhood training gave him the strength and perseverance not only to work his way through college in Colorado and the Harvard Medical School, but also while doing so to send some little financial aid to help his father's family. So, it would seem that the Amish way may also afford very excellent discipline to prepare a young man for life even among the non-Amish.

The pictures which follow are the fruit of our years of association with the Amish.

KIEHL NEWSWANGER

Lancaster
Pennsylvania

AMISHLAND

AT SCHOOL
Onn's Schuul

SCREAMS, giggles and shouts could be heard for some distance, just like in any young children's recess period, but here at the little one-room Amish schoolhouse known as Snake Hill the students are different.

The boys all wear the same broadbrimmed flat hats, suspendered trousers and brilliant homemade shirts as their grown up parents do.

Yonnie Lapp, just six years old, and his first year at school, has on in miniature the attire of his father, Chris, and great-grandfather Jacob, who incidentally had given the land from the corner of his field for the Amish schoolhouse.

The girls are all neat as pins with their smocks, and pigtails in a net, and the older girls with the neat blue and gray aprons and prayer caps.

Today my father and I came over for a visit, and of course the older boys had to have us "in the mush," the "It" of corner ball, *eck balle* the favorite Amish sport. There are two teams of four, one boy in each corner throwing a ball at the dodging team of four in the center, until all are hit and eliminated. After dodging and twisting for ten minutes, Jake Speicher finally winged me a good hard smack in the back, but our team out-lasted his.

Just then the Amish "tietscher" *schuulmeisterin* Miss Beiler rang the school bell which hangs suspended in the quaint little bell tower.

The fourth graders were reciting their lesson in front of the blackboard, occasionally prompted by Miss Beiler. When they wrote their sums on the board, no English school could find brighter pupils.

David Smucker could divide and multiply and figure sums in his head in a

flash *geschwind wie en wedder-laich*. I always laugh when I think of his remark about Elmer his brother who was a little backward in school. In Dutch: "It ain't he can't learn, it's just that after he learns it, he forgets it." *Siss net ass er es net larna konn, juisht er fargisst grawd.*

Little Katie was in her first year too. She just loved to play with the girls, swinging on the turnstile and with Yonnie, the shy first grader. Every day she'd bring her bright red reader home, mostly I think because she liked the cover, with a gold picture of a sailing ship.

16

This school goes to eight grades, after which the children will stay home and take over more full-time chores.

The boys, if not needed at home, hire out to other Amish. Sometimes the girls do too.

Since my first visit at the school, David Smucker and Levina Esch have married and settled in Mose Glick's tenant house and it won't be too many years until they have a shy little first grader like Yonnie — lunch kettle in hand, running in from recess when Miss Beiler rings the Old Snake Hill bell.

"It ain't he can't learn, its just that
after he learns it, he forgets it."

YONNIE LAPP SCHOOLBOY
Schuulbuu

HERE is Yonnie Lapp. It's his first day at school and even the little one-room school *schuulhaus* with the pillared porch seems big to him.

After he saw his own small wooden desk with the fancy black metal legs, the long new yellow pencils, and the gaily colored crayon drawings over the top of the windows, he knew he'd like it there.

At lunch *middawg* Miss Beiler, the Amish *tietscher,* showed him how to toast his sandwiches over the stove grate, using the long iron toaster.

At recess he played tag with the second grade *maydels,* most of whom he knew.

Now on his way home after the first day with his new blue reader, he's no longer the strange, shy first grader.

21

KATIE GLICK SCHOOLGIRL

Schuulmaydel

KATIE GLICK is on her way home from school. She is in the second grade this year and is a good little pupil — especially in reading.

Katie is David's oldest daughter. Each year these past four years David has had a new daughter. Finally this year Sarah presented him with a son Jacob, named after his grandfather Jake Glick, our butcher.

A son is a necessary thing on the farm, otherwise David would have to always keep a hired boy or depend on help from his sons-in-law when his daughters married.

Katie is a beautiful blond little girl. I always recall her playing with her little wide-eyed sister Barbie, just three, as if she were a doll — putting on her little bonnet and lifting her into the cart in the yard, exclaiming, "Now we will go to market." *Now gayn mer an der marrick.*

Every day on her way home from school she'd stop at Amos's place. He would take her into the corner of the cow stable and proudly show her the furry little guinea pigs he was raising. She loved to play with the little animals and the day Amos sold them and bought rabbits, she cried. But it wasn't long before she became fascinated by the big white, long-eared rabbits.

Katie was old Jake's favorite little grandchild and most every nice day he'd drive his open spring wagon (usually full of three or four other grandchildren) up for Katie and take her down to his small farm where she'd romp and play with her cousins and sit on her Grosse Daddy's knee.

*The girls are all neat as pins
with their smocks.*

THE AMISH CARPENTERS

Schreiner

THE hardest job of putting up Mose Riehl's barn was the foundation.

Mose used the regular field stone which he had been gathering up ever since he had started farming the place.

Joe Riehl, Mose's brother and his other Amish carpenters, including me, would be there every morning at six-thirty to begin the arduous job of breaking up the large rock into workable pieces, mixing the countless buckets of mortar and being the masons.

Preacher Mose (he was the preacher in that district), was a large robust man with hands like hams and a build like Atlas.

He would pick up the heavy sledge-hammer and give the rock a terrific smack, sending it into about four pieces. Then he picked up the largest, weighing about one hundred pounds and carried it to the foundation site as though it were a pebble.

This field stone retained moisture and would make a fine potato celler or hanging place for tobacco.

Speaking of foundations, when I worked with Mose he told me about an Amishman named Wiry Jake who got that name because he used wire from hay bales to fix anything that was broken around his farm. Well, it seems he purchased an old trolley car to convert into a chicken house. He measured it off first, then went home and built a foundation for it. When he finally had it moved to the new foundation, it was a few feet too long. He quizzically scratched his head and exclaimed, "By dingity, I thought I stepped that off right." *Ich hop gedenkt daas ich recht oppschtept hopp bei gumm.*

After our ten-foot foundation walls were completed and when the oak timbers had arrived from western Pennsylvania, we began the work of measuring off the beams and braces, chiseling out the setting holes, cutting the tenons to fit into them and making the peg holes. We did this all using only two-man saws, an adz and our hand tools.

In about ten days the timbers were ready for the barn raising.

At six o'clock on a still-dawning June morning, Amish buggies began arriving at Mose's place.

We had already laid a rough floor on the foundation.

Three gangs of twenty or more carried the heavy beams on to the floor where our boss carpenters made sure the frames were assembled correctly. Then up with the first frame.

It reminded me of hoisting up huge granite blocks when the first Gothic cathedrals were built by inspired artisans.

Seventy or eighty Amish were pushing up the frame into position, some using long pike poles while others on the opposite side pulled on the ropes tied to the frame. A little jockeying back and forth and it fell into place and was quickly braced up.

When one of the end frames was going up, the pegs twisted loose from one end of it and sent Johnathan Zook, who had been riding it up in order to brace it, crashing to the boards below. Luckily the beam crashing down with him missed his head but it looked like he had a badly broken leg.

The Amish are physically brave and I've never seen one flinch or break down.

The following week at a Georgetown raising, an Amishman was killed when a timber fell on him.

Working with such heavy timbers, the Amish are fortunate not to have more accidents, but then, all of them are experienced carpenters as they do most of their own building and repair work.

We had the frame all up by noon with the help of some mid-morning sandwiches and lemonade which the visiting women brought to us.

After the usual barn raising feast, we started the sheathing and bracing up.

By five that afternoon, we had all the side sheathing on, part of the roof, and in another week the regular carpenters would have it completed.

Standing in the huge shell of the barn that evening, I marveled at what the combined efforts of these Amish neighbors could accomplish in a few well-directed hours.

While I was working at Mose's place I also heard another story from the tall Amish carpenter Elam Zook. It seems that he and Eli Esch had to build an out-house once at Bauweller's. They were getting along good with it till they got to the seat holes. Eli got a big smile on his face and said he'd a sure fire way of getting them figured right. He was going to fetch Emma and set her on the seat and mark around her with his pencil!

THE BUTCHER JACOB GLICK

Der Bootcher

IT was Saturday and another market day for my friend Jacob Glick. Saturday was Jake's big market day at the Southern Market in Lancaster just south of our old Penn Square.

Every Friday and Saturday I drove him and his meat products in to the market. Ten or fifteen years ago Jake would probably have driven his own market wagon into the town, but now he seldom did, not only because it took longer, but now with the building of new highways into the city it just isn't safe to be on the same road with our high-powered autos. Many Amish have been killed while driving their wagons on the main roads.

He'd still peddle to the farms and out-lying villages in his wagon; and many a day I peddled peaches with his son David in the country districts.

It was always pleasant for me to drive the old spring wagon; so much closer to nature than driving an auto, and I could catch all the sweet summer fragrances.

I was up at his farm at five to help load his succulent hams, *schunkefleesch* long sticks of Lebanon *baluunie,* tripe *kuudelfleck* and cup cheese *kupp kais.*

On the way in we stopped at Katie Stoltzfus's to pick up her load of eighty brown loaves which she had baked on the day before in the old brick oven in David's kettle house *kesselhous.*

It was a brisk October morning, but by ten o'clock the bright sun shone warmly through the high Gothic windows of the Southern Market.

The stalls, with the home-grown flowers, reminded me of the colorful mid-summer market days.

If my readers have never seen a Lancaster Market, there is a rare sight in store for them. The high beamed ceiling and the Gothic windows, with the soft dusty light filtering through them, remind one of an old-world cathedral.

Jake's stall was in the first aisle across from Melinda Esch's flower and plant stand. Melinda's bright yellow chrysanthemums and colorful leafed colia emerged in sharp contrast to the somber brown stall and grey brick wall behind her.

Next to Jake was old Mose and Naomi Lapp with their butter, eggs, and fat and tender friers.

On down the aisle past Elam Riehl's cabbages were all kinds of mixed potato salads *grumbeer Salawd* then past Issac Glick's cheese stall and the tempting *Schweitzerkais* made at the Amish Cheese Factory near Intercourse.

On Saturday young Melinda and Barbara Stoltzfus would help Jake sell his products, not only the hams and *baluunie,* but Katie's bread and bright red winesaps which David and I had picked that week.

Old Jake with his yellowish-white patriarchal beard, his broadbrim hat and dark green shirt, would deftly slice thick red cuts from his home-cured hams.

Watching him work in front of the market stall amid the shadows cast from the wide shelves above him, brought to mind St. Peter coming out of the catacombs.

Old Jake had many friends, not only among the Amish, but with outsiders who were attracted to him by his kindliness, softspokenness and his uncommon good sense which all seemed to spring from his faith in God and man.

Just last month Jake died and never will I visit the market without thinking of old Jake the butcher, a simple man, and truly a man of God.

BREAD BAKING KATIE STOLTZFUS
Brot Bocke

IT was a cool June evening as Katie Stoltzfus opened her oven door in the *kesselhous* and drew out the last batch of forty round loaves of bread. She had been baking since six o'clock this morning in order to have her eighty loaves for tomorrow's market at Lancaster.

First she had made the dough *hut der dayk schaaft* —kneading it in the old kneading tray—then cut it into forty pieces, rolling them into shape, and put them into the greased pans to raise for an hour, while she started the oven fire from the pile of kindling and chunks that little Katie had neatly piled against the oven.

On Thursdays, while the first batch was baking, she'd do her house work.

She and Melinda, her unmarried daughter, lived in a separate part of David Glick's house. She had come to live with her eldest married daughter, David's wife, ten years ago after her own husband had been trampled to death by a runaway horse.

She'd sweep the porches, beat the rag rugs, perhaps make a few pies to put in the oven after the last batch of bread.

I was in the kettle house as she took the last batch out of the oven, using the long peel *shooter*. All the loaves were a beautiful golden brown, filling the room with their appetizing odor. With a weary sigh she banged the heavy oven door shut and said in Dutch someday she'd stop baking *sie dait mal stoppen bocke*, but I knew it was a part of her weekly work and after thirty years of baking every Thursday she'd not stop now even though she was past sixty.

On other nights through the week she'd sit on her porch and peel apples for *schnitzing* and I'd take them over to Peanut (I don't know how this Amishman got that nickname) Esch's *schnitzing* oven to be dried out and hung in bags in the attic until winter, to be used to make Katie's tempting pies *boie*.

It was about twelve o'clock when Katie finished buttering the tops of the loaves to give them an extra shininess and flavor. Then, taking long muslin cloths, she tenderly draped them over the loaves as though she was tucking her children in for the night.

THE CARPET WEAVER

Karapet Wayver

GROSSE MENNO STOLTZFUS

I SAW the storm lantern burning in big Menno Stoltzfus's weave shop in back of his house as I drove in the lane with two large bags of different colored rags for rugs.

It was a warm June evening and Menno was hard at work on his loom making the shuttle go back and forth.

As his name implies, he was a huge man with large features. His hat seemed more like a round cap with a brim on his large head than the broadbrimmed affair it actually was.

Sitting on the bench in front of his loom (his grandfather Aaron had made it over eighty years ago), he seemed to dwarf everything in the shop.

I carried the two bags in to him.

Standing in the dim light behind their father's bench, I saw his two little boys. Benuel, the elder boy, would kneel down and rapidly refill the shuttle from the spools of different colored rags lined up under the bench. Little Samuel stayed noiselessly against the shed's side wall watching the shuttle weave back and forth.

Menno gave me a nod of hello when I entered and kept on working.

I had known Menno when I had worked with the Amish carpenters remodeling his horse stable. He would come into the stable in the morning where we were replacing the weak timbers, nod to us and we wouldn't see him again till the evening feeding when he would again nod to us. He was truly a man of few words.

This evening, for some reason, he seemed talkative and told me he was just finishing up the rug runner for his son's new bride, Rachel King. Perhaps the pride of having a daughter-in-law brought about this unusual loquacity.

Menno was not only a weaver of rugs (mostly rag rugs for the Amish), but he also ran his one-hundred-acre farm; he did most of his weaving in the evenings.

Although his father and grandfather had both been weavers, he had only been doing it since he bought the family farm some ten years ago.

He had learned to weave as a child and perhaps he had started it again partly because he wanted to put the old loom to use; and then it gave him some-

thing to do during his odd hours. Although, with all the wedding orders for next November, he was kept too busy and very seldom read his Martyr's book which as a young man he would read and reread for an hour or more every night.

I told Menno how long a rug I wanted and to start it and end it with a blue strip; and with a nod and a wave goodnight, he picked up the shuttle and resumed work.

Looking at him through the shop window as I drove out, reminded me of a country organist practicing his organ late on a Saturday evening.

THE COBBLER MOSE BEILER

Schuumacher

MOSE BEILER, the cobbler at Intercourse, had never taken to farming very much. Although as a younger man he had hired out on neighboring farms and then as a married man he worked for his father-in-law Jake Petersheim back of Bird-in-Hand.

When Joe Riehl started his carpenter gang Mose was quick to get a job with them. He had always been handy with a hammer and saw and within a year he was what we call a finished carpenter doing all the inside and trim work, hanging doors and everything that required a skilled hand.

When he moved into Intercourse, he decided to open up a little shoe repair shop in the front of his house which was across from Intercourse Bank.

His shop reminded me of a Rembrandt print, with deep shadows cutting back and forth across the dusty line of repaired shoes and the fancily carved clock on the wall. I always remember Mose sitting on his cobbler's bench in his brilliant blue homemade shirt—a stout, good hearted man with a twinkle in his eye (in fact he loved to play practical jokes on our carpenter gang and whenever an Amishman found his broadbrimmed hat nailed to the floor or tried to get up from fitting a piece of flooring and found his pants nailed fast, Mose was sure to have had a hand in it).

Mose never had any children of his own, but he loved them, and whenever a little Amish boy or girl would come in from the schoolyard which was next to his shop, they were sure to leave with a bit of gum or candy or laughing over some joke or "tease" Mose had made.

HORSESHOEING
Om Gaul Schlaage

THE timeless sound of metal on metal made my ears ring as I approached the Amish blacksmith shop back of the general store in Smoketown. It was a cold February morning and the wind was picking up clouds of snow which had fallen during the night and was swirling them around the corner of the old frame blacksmith shop. A great-coated Amishman was leading his black horse out of the shop door across the white snow. The Amishman with his bushy black beard and the dark flowing cape (which was added to his great-coat for warmth), reminded me of some old piece of Chinese sculpture as he hitched his horse to his market wagon.

The Amish take very good care of their horses' feet as most all the roads are "tarred" now and hard on a horse's tender hooves.

I entered the shop and said goodday to the smith Jake Lapp, who was skilfully pounding a horseshoe into shape on his anvil. His young son Eli was vigorously pumping the bellows for him. In one corner of the shop, quietly holding a big brown mare's head I recognized my carpenter friend, old Dave Zook. While working, old "talky" Jake, as we had nicknamed him, kept up a steady stream of conversation (all in Dutch) about everything: the rising price of grain; what he got for his tobacco last year; the coming Thursday cow sale at New Holland; the heavy snow we had last week. I was glad when Dick, the horse (the Amish give their horses and cows very simple names like Bill and Dick and Sally) gave a startled jump just as a piece of hot coal hit his rump, and Jake stopped talking for a few minutes. Dave and I both held Dick as Jake rasped down the hoof so the shoe would fit smoothly against it.

Jake was a talker, and even with his mouth full of shoe nails he started off on his steady stream: the new school board; local politics; that Korea war; even asked me what I thought of the Russians when I was in Odessa a few years back. He was a funny little man with a short red beard and bright shiny eyes—and a limp from when he was kicked by a horse as a boy apprentice in his father's shop.

The horse was shod, and as we led him out the door Dave and I winked at each other. It was good to inhale the crisp air after the strong smell of burnt hoof, and the incessant talk of "talky" Jake. But he was a good smith and very seldom did a horse lose one of his shoes put on by old Jake Lapp the Smoketown blacksmith.

THE CARRIAGE MAKER

Kootchmocher

JONATHAN STOLTZFUS

JONATHAN STOLTZFUS' carriage shop *weggeli schopp* is in the little village of Monterey on the main road that leads to Intercourse (the center of the Amish settlement in Lancaster County). Many years ago he had bought the shop from his cousin Isaac Stoltzfus, the Amish bee keeper *iem haalter* and he had started it out as a kind of tool shop for sharpening all kinds of saws, axes, mowers and other metal utensils used by his farm neighbors. Besides this business, he worked his own small farm, and raised several hundred chickens every year.

Whenever an Amish wagon or buggy wheel would need repairing, it would be brought to him, so gradually he began repairing and building new Amish buggies until today most all his work is wagon building, and he is teaching his oldest son Joseph the trade.

It is a long and tedious job building an Amish buggy. All the different wooden parts of the buggy are fitted and bolted together with the same care and skill that a cabinet maker uses. Jonathan made everything for his buggies except the shafts and wheels, which he bought from Philadelphia. As the Amish are not permitted to have electricity, all the machines he worked with were run by small gasoline engines.

The evening I took my saw and hatchet down to him to be sharpened it was dark in his shop except for one corner where, by lantern light, he was grinding down an axe. I could see many sparks flying off from the grinding stone, sometimes half lighting up all the corners of his rear shop. Bending over his work, with his graying red beard and deeply lined face, he looked like a man out of a Rembrandt portrait, with only the yellow lantern lighting his face and hands, and the rest of his body lost in the darkness of the shop.

Seeing me he looked up and smiling said, "I'm sharpening up the axe for tomorrow's chicken corn soup." *Ich mach de ax scharf far hinkel-welschkorn suppe far moya.* I showed him my dull axe and saw, and with a wry smile, while squinting down the saw teeth, he asked me if I had sawed many nails with it. Jokingly, I said, "Only small ones."

Before leaving, he took me over to one corner of his shop and showed me a new Amish buggy which was almost finished except for the coats of shiny black paint and the gray canvas paint for the buggy's top. As he lit the way for me across the hard packed dirt floor of the shop, I noticed a partly demolished Amish buggy. It seemed that last Sunday night an auto had collided with the buggy and had thrown the young Amish boy into the gutter. Luckily he hit the soft dirt sidebank, although the horse was killed and it would cost some two hundred dollars to repair the buggy.

Outside in the driveway we both laughed when we saw his two youngest children sitting in the front seat of my jeep, curiously examining the many buttons, and occasionally pushing the shrill horn. Going out the drive I waved goodbye to Jonathan, who with a child in each arm was going up into his kerosene-lit kitchen.

It is a long and tedious job
building an Amish weggele.

SPRING PLOWING

Om Frieyawr Blooga

ANOTHER spring had come to the flat fields around the small Amish community of Intercourse.

In most every field, an Amishman or boy was seen walking behind his plow with the same tireless, long, plowing gait.

Going through this landscape one sensed the awakening of life from its winter sleep.

Newborn colts were frisking with their mothers, the bleating of young lambs and the shrill cry of the heifers mingled in the meadows and the crow-cawing was heard from the fields where the tender green shoots of winter wheat were growing almost while you watched them.

Elam Esch and his two sons, Henner (Henry) and Johnathan, were tirelessly plowing, each with a separate team.

Elam liked to walk along behind his faithful horses, Jack and Bill, watching the earth turned over on the same farm his great-grandfather Elijah had cleared from the then thick wilderness.

Elam could hear the noise of his "Englisha" neighbor's tractor sputtering in the distance. It certainly did the work a lot faster, but then Elam liked the feel of the reins across his shoulder and the horse smell and the occasional spark when the plow hit a piece of flint stone. No, his old-fashioned way was more the way God wanted it.

Seeing him with the wind blowing his long beard across his neck reminded me of an old Yankee sea captain at the wheel on a wind-swept day.

His team skillfully manipulated the turns at the end of the field with a word of command, "Gee" or "Haw."

Elam tied his team up to the cherry tree alongside the road when he saw me arrive with his bags of fertilizer.

Wiping the sweat from his brow, he exclaimed, "It's hot!" *Siss heiss!* in spite of the cool spring breeze.

Reaching up he snapped off a twig of the cherry blossoms and with a smile held their sweet fragrance under my nose.

Seeing his horses starting to kick and stomp at the tree Elam had to leave me and return to his task.

Hearing the mid-day dinner bell clanging across the fields I envied Elam the hearty Amish dinner *'s grosse esse* that awaited him in the kitchen.

42

THE SOWER

Der Sayer

AN amusing incident occurred one Spring day shortly after I had returned from the cattle trip to Europe.

Ben Smucker, our Amish neighbor who was sowing clover among the winter wheat across from our place, stopped at our pump house for a drink of water and while he was there he got to asking us about the ocean. He said he had been talking to Tommy Lapp and wondered why the ocean didn't make a sharp turn aways out. He couldn't visualize a round earth, but rather imagined a series of sharp turns. I told him about the horizon and that the world had a very slow curve the whole way around because of its size.

Ben had also been unable to imagine the idea of an eclipse and actually seeing the earth's shadow on the moon.

The Amish read and believe the Bible literally: they accept all miracles, believe without question that men have lived to be hundreds of years old; but the everyday wonders of science seem strange and unbelieveable to them.

But then they don't need this knowledge, and it doesn't prevent them from being the best farmers in Lancaster County.

HOEING CORN
Om Welschkorn Hocka*

THIS is Levina Esch, Elam's older sister, hoeing in the cornfield on a hot July day. There has been a lot of rain through June and even though David cultivated it with the horse every week, the weeds kept popping up. Now it was too high for the horse and cultivator to get through, so it all had to be hoed by hand.

After Levina had helped her mother clear off the breakfast dishes and wash out the milk pails, she donned her red kerchief and spent three or four hours hoeing.

She'd only hoe in the forenoon, as the sun would sometimes become unbearable in the afternoon and we could see heat waves rising from the cornfields as it baked out the damp red earth.

On summer afternoons she'd play in the yard swing under the pear tree, sometimes weed the garden or play in the barn with Elam.

Today she was going down to Amos's place to the quilting party with her mother, Sabina. She liked that, as she'd see Naomi and Anna Mary and together they'd romp through the big apple orchard, climb the trees and pull their play wagon through the shaded orchard grass.

This was her last year at the one-room school. Next year she was going to hire out with her brother-in-law, Solomon King, down at Churchtown, and help her eldest sister Mary keep house and tend her new baby girl.

★ "Welsch" in German means "foreign"; Indian corn or maize was new to the Pennsylvania Dutch settlers and is therefore "foreign" corn, to distinguish it from ordinary "corn," the German word for wheat and grain generally.

HOEING TOBACCO
Om Duuwack Hocka

EVERY nice September day before the tobacco was cut, little Elam Esch, in the third grade at the Snake Hill School, would hoe tobacco in the afternoon.

He'd walk home from school every day with his older sister Levina and little Amos Glick who had just started school this year. They'd stop along the way to pick goldenrod and sometimes explore in the old abandoned mill at Eden and run back and forth in the dried up mill stream.

Today Elam was hungry as usual, and after a big slice of his mother's homemade bread with a spoonful of tangy dark brown applebutter *eppel buutter* he went out to the chicken house where he kept his small hoe.

His married brother Abner had cut down the handle on a big hoe and ground the metal part down to just the right size and weight for little Elam.

Before going up to the tobacco field he always climbed the steps to the loft over the chicken house to feed his pigeons. Elam now had fourteen pigeons. He sold the young ones for squabs and kept two pairs for breeding.

Every week after Saturday market his mother would give him his squab money and he would give it to his father to save for him to buy a shiny buggy *glitzerische weggele* when he was sixteen.

Elam liked to hoe tobacco. In fact, being smaller, he could easily reach under the big tender leaves and chop out any weeds.

Today he found a big green tobacco worm almost three inches long. A whopper! *n' verdeiwelte grosser!* He carefully slipped it into his pocket until he could get a jar for it later.

At four o'clock (five, our time, as the Amish always go on slow or standard time) the supper bell rang.

Today he had finished two long rows and in another week he would be helping his father cut and harvest this valuable crop.

SPEARING TOBACCO

Om Duuwack Eifeddla

SPEARING tobacco correctly is a trick that not everyone can get onto.

Watching Levi Petersheim spear was a study in motion.

Paul, his brother-in-law, and I were going along cutting the tall stalks so they'd wilt for a while in the hot sun, making them easier and lighter to spear.

Levi would pick up a plant—at the same time put the metal spear on the end of the four-foot lath, and with a quick movement pierce the center of the stalk and send it down the lath—as he picked up another plant with his right hand.

We generally put five plants on one lath, but this summer, as they were extra large, we only put four to a lath.

Little Isaac went along in front of Levi with an armful of laths bigger than himself dropping one lath every four plants.

After we had about half an acre of the ten-acre patch cut, Paul and I started to spear. We both started in line with Levi, but spearing as fast as we knew how, we still couldn't keep up with him. He called back jokingly in Dutch if we felt ill today *Feelscht net gute heit?*

His hired boy, Elias King, and his daughter Sadie loaded the filled laths onto the wagon and took them into the tobacco shed. Every other load either Paul or I would drive the big mule team into the shed where we'd unload the heavy laths.

When we started at the shed's peak, Linda would take the laths on which the tobacco hung off the back end of the wagon, hand a lath overhead to me, then I'd walk catlike on a rafter and shove one end of the lath up to Elias who was perched on a board a good fifty feet from the barn floor—no place for people who are bothered by height. Most all the Amish are athletic and can climb around in high places "where angels fear to tread," as they announce about circus high wire artists.

Hanging tobacco can be dangerous at times if one should slip from his perch or a rafter slip out of place.

One day a rafter full of tobacco splintered in the middle and came crashing down to the barn floor barely missing my father who was unloading tobacco under it.

That year I worked a month in the hot late August sun, putting away the ten acres and it was work cutting, spearing and hanging that heavy tobacco crop.

IN THE TOBACCO STRIPPING ROOM

Duuwack

Schtripping Schtuub

JANUARY was the bleakest month for me on the farm. Through the day I would help David Glick do the regular farm chores—feed, milk and clean out the stalls. On days that weren't too blustery or snowy we would haul out manure to leach through the earth over the winter, making it rich and productive.

On those cold nights we all gathered in the stripping room under the *forebay* (overhang of the barn) to strip the tobacco off their stalks and sort the different sizes.

As I pushed open the old battened door (which slammed shut by the weight of six horseshoes tied to a rope through a pulley) the warm air from the chunk stove blew up in my wind-burned face and I inhaled the acrid smells of damp tobacco.

Katie, Melinda, David and I stood at the long workbench and as we stripped off the dampened leaves (tobacco must be sprinkled first so it won't crumble when handled), we sorted them into seven different sized wooden trays on the wide workbench which ran around two sides of the little room. When we had enough ready to make a bale *duuwacksbindel* of about eighty pounds, I would carefully place the leaves in the old wooden baler and press the bales together about the size of a hay bale, tie them up and carry them to the barn floor above us.

Occasionally small bits of tobacco leaves would get in our eyes. What a sting! *es beisst!* and we'd jump for the water bucket kept in the corner for such an emergency.

It was always dark outside when we stripped tobacco and this particular night snow started to fall again and, driven by a high wind, it banged against our windows and reminded me of my sailing days when the winds beat on my cabin portholes while inside we felt like animals burrowed in for the winter— warm and secure but still respecting the elements.

Old Katie, our bread baker, was past sixty, but when it came to sorting tobacco she outdid us all. Nimbly her small gnarled hands stripped the stalks, sorted them and picked up another with her left hand without even a break.

Young Linda was standing stolidly on the packed ground floor humming almost inaudibly one of the German hymns.

David and I talked incessantly in low tones, most about horses. David loved trotters and if he hadn't been an Amishman he would most likely have been a breeder of horses; in fact he still raised five or six colts just for the pleasure of seeing them grow and breaking them to the harness.

We all laughed as David lifted one of the little grey kittens off the floor and put it into Linda's sorting tray while she was bending over to pick up some leaves.

I had just finished packing our third bale when Katie and Melinda said *guut naacht* and, glancing at the clock, David said, "It's ten o'clock and time for bed." *Siss tzaia ur un tzeit fer uns nesht.*

We put out the storm lantern, closed the damper on the chunk stove and ran to the house through the dark, windy cold.

CORN CUTTING AT SNAKE HILL
Welschkorn Opphocka

'LL never forget the first week of corn cutting in September, with Mose Glick, and his sons, John, Chris and David, on their farms over near the little one-room Amish schoolhouse, known as Snake Hill School. The Amish are about the only farmers in Lancaster County who still cut corn by hand. Chris' corn field was about a third of a mile long, running from the end of his meadow to the woods behind David's orchard. I had just returned from my annual visit to Sarasota and I was a little out of shape, at least, for corn cutting.

Well I've never gotten into shape faster. We started out with corn cutters swinging (these are somewhat similar to a machete with a leather thong to slip around the wrist). The sun had only been up about a half hour, so after the first row our pants were soaked to the skin from the heavy early dew which clung, like silver threads, to the corn stalks. None of us wore shoes, and the soft red soil would keep sticking to our toes. By midday we wished the early morning wetness would have stayed with us. Back and forth we went making piles of ten or twelve stalks to be loaded onto the corn wagons and hauled into the cutter and blown up into Chris' tall silo, to be used for his winter silage for cow feed. Old Mose, who is past sixty, kept right up with us. After five straight hours in the morning sun, I was certainly glad to hear the dinner bell.

DINNER AFTER CORN CUTTING
Mittdawgesse Nach Welschkorn Opphocka

I HAVE a reputation for being a big eater among the Amish, so after washing and exchanging merriments (mostly about the rip in Jake Speicher's pants which he tore on a corn stubble) we went into the kitchen (which is the main living room for the entire Amish family).

After a solemn silent prayer of almost a minute, we started in on what the English would consider a feast *'s grosse esse*. First, gravied (dippy) beef, bologna *baluunie,* cup cheese *kupp kais,* mashed potatoes *grumbeere sas,* succotash, chow chow, apple sauce *eppel sas,* cole slaw *graut selawd,* tomatoes *tomats* peas *arrobsa,* pickled beets and eggs *rote riewa oier,* milked crackers *milch grackers* and the dessert although it all seemed to run together, peaches *paasching,* banana pudding, blackberry mush *blockberre mush,* jello, chocolate cake *chocklawt kuuche, schnitz* pie and various jams and condiments I won't mention for fear of making my readers hungry.

The only trouble with the Amish is that they are all such fast eaters and usually finish off in about twenty minutes. I had learned long ago to forsake polite conversation.

The Amishman next to me, Jonnie Lapp, ate one thing at a time. First he heaped his plate with mashed potatoes and gravy, then meat, then vegetables, etc.

The Amish are quite polite eaters, although it is alright to eat with a spoon, probably because most of their meats and vegetables are prepared with thin sauces and gravies.

After the cake and pies have made their final rounds, Mose says: "If everyone has had enough, let's pray." *Wonn mer sott sin, wull mer baida.* And we bow our heads in silent grace. *Gott's donk.*

The Amish always have grace before and after every meal.

The Amish women who had been serving us, then sat down to eat before clearing off the table.

Going out, Mose, seeing that I had difficulty walking, said, "Well, Chris, now you'll be able to work," *Now kanscht schaffe, Grischt* and in ten minutes we were hard at it.

GATHERING POTATOES

Om Grumbeere Uffleesa

YONNIE KING, the hired boy, had raked the potato vines off the field the day before the Beilers, Chris, his wife, Sarah, and two sons, Levi and Reuben, started to pick potatoes.

In spite of the light rain which had fallen during the night, the ground was not too wet to begin early in the morning.

Chris's field was on a high hill overlooking the big stone barn and the old plastered house of stone. Looking down from the field a whole landscape panorama unfolded. To the left, beside the house, was a clump of tall, green pines. Behind the bank barn (the upper part of the barn which is banked up so that wagons can pull up into it) was the luxuriant meadow with the meadow stream lined on either side with the graceful meadow trees. Thirty or more Holstein cows were peacefully grazing and several hundred white Leghorn chickens were scratching around their summer houses. The hard road twisted through the fields like a snake and seemed to stop abruptly where the woods on the high hill met the sky. The entire background had the appearance of a stage set.

Even little Chris helped with the potatoes. Only eight years old, he drove the horse and long wagon which carried the empty baskets to the pickers and took the full ones back to the barn floor where Levi and Reuben emptied them into the burlap sacks to be stored in the potato cellar under the tobacco shed until sold next month.

Potato picking, like tomato picking, is a break-back job. Constantly bending over, cleaning the roots of their solid brown harvest, big Chris worked tirelessly.

Barefooted, with a light blue shirt, jet black beard and deep pink skin, he seemed to be a part of the rich earth.

Sarah, wearing a pink dress, blue apron and kerchief around her hair, looked like one of Millet's French peasant drawings.

Little Melinda walked silently behind her Mother's basket and kept picking up the little marble-sized potatoes which Sarah had left discarded on the vines. In a few years she would be picking in earnest beside her mother.

Just then I heard a loud bang! I thought perhaps a horse had taken off, but only a bag had split open while being lifted down and sent potatoes crashing on the barn floor. Chris, with a sly scowl, looked up to say how the bags were getting so loosely woven compared to the old ones that could hold water.

The upper five-acre field yielded 2250 bushels—a good harvest and profit for Chris. With a good corn harvest in sight he could afford to buy the new thrashing rig now, and perhaps add a steer shed onto the barn.

We had almost finished picking the small lower field when dark clouds suddenly blew over the entire sky and thunder rumbled, and big pellets of rain came dashing down on us from this Indian summer rain storm.

We all made a dash for the barn floor and spent the last hour until dusk filling the bags and tying them up with twine.

Just before the sunset the clouds cleared and we saw a *marrick warrich* (wonderful) rainbow arc across the sky.

PEACH PICKING
Om Paasching Ruppa

I GET hungry whenever I think of peach picking up at David Glick's orchard in early August. Davey was like me and loved to eat them. We'd pick a few, eat one, then pick another and eat two more succulent Alberta peaches. There would usually be four of us picking: Barbara Stoltzfus, David's young cousin, old Amos King, and Katie Stoltzfus, David's mother-in-law.

The first thing we would do on these shining August mornings would be to hitch up Barney, the big horse, to the long spring wagon; then we'd go into the old frame tool shed and load several dozen peach baskets onto it and drive through the meadow up to the upper orchard. Old Jake, David's father, had planted the trees when he was a young man, and with careful pruning, spraying and fertilizing they had yielded a good crop every year.

This full-sized orchard, along with the regular crops, kept David and his family very busy during harvest. Every day was a long and full one for David: up at four-thirty; milk the cows from five till six before the dairyman came to pick up the filled milk cans; clean out the horse and cow stalls; and on market days drive his wife and father into the Lancaster market and sometimes "stand market" with them; then in the later morning, cultivate corn or hoe tobacco till late afternoon when the cows had to be driven in from pasture, milked and fed again; perhaps take a calf or other animal down to the New Holland sales barn. By nine these hard-working Amish folk are ready for bed. And the women too are hard workers. Besides keeping a neat house and garden, canning, making most of the family's clothes, it is not uncommon to see them working in the harvest alongside the men; spearing tobacco; hanging it; getting in the potato and fruit harvest. Melinda, Sarah's youngest sister, could spear tobacco as fast as any of the Amish menfolk (besides baking the best layer cake I'd ever tasted).

David didn't have any grown sons yet to work the farm, but with the women folk all helping at harvest time he was able to keep ahead of the ripening crops.

This particular morning we had to pick extra fast as David wanted some forty baskets to peddle around the neighboring countryside that afternoon. By ten o'clock the hot sun was beating down on us and quickly dried out the heavy dew that covers the ground on these summer mornings. David had already shed his shoes and while I was taking mine off he laughingly threw a hard peach stone which made me jump and let out a loud "ouch!" By noon we had picked some

forty-odd baskets. Both David's and my shirt were in rips in the back from the jagged peach branches. We jumped on the spring wagon, and without guiding Barney, he trotted us back to the barn. Barney knew the orchard by heart; on some evenings when we had picked late and it was pitch black in the orchard, Barney would knowingly trot us back to the barn, missing the almost invisible trees and stumps.

That afternoon David and I peddled our peaches in the small towns and farms in that district. Coming home at dusk we had sold every basket and didn't even have one juicy peach to eat on the homeward trot.

THRESHING AT R. AMOS GLICK'S
Om Drescha bei R. Amos Glick

IT was sweltering on that early July day in R. Amos Glick's wheat field, but the weather was right for threshing.

All the Glicks were there. Amos U. Glick, his cousin Amos S. and R. Amos (they all used the extra initial because their given names were the same) and his sons, Steffy and Aaron.

Aaron had never joined the church, much to the sorrow of his father, old Amos. He had become too interested in cars and when he became twenty-one, he bought a car with his tobacco money. Of course he couldn't keep it at home, so he garaged it over in Leola.

Not too many years ago he would not have been permitted to live at home after that but now, even among the Amish, the rules are a little less strict.

Old Amos had given up talking to Aaron about his dressing. Aaron is changing from an Amishman, but his father still hopes that someday Aaron will see his folly and come back to the church.

It seemed so incongruous at dinner to see Aaron beardless, sporting a necktie and close haircut, sitting next to his Amish brother Stephen who reminded me of one of the young Apostles.

It was a loss for the farm too, as Aaron had taken a job at the linoleum factory in Lancaster in order to save for a new car and pay for its upkeep.

Aaron could spear tobacco faster than anyone around Zook's corner and he was able to cap wheat better than most and he had the strength of two mules.

The thresher was on the barn floor and we had three wagons in the field picking up the sheaves *die schayf rei' bringen.*

Old Amos drove the team. Young Eli was on the wagon and Steffy and I pitched the sheaves up with our long forks *pitchgawwel.*

There was hardly a breeze and the sweat was pouring from us.

Steffy wore only an undershirt which is unusual as the Amish are very modest and seldom go shirtless.

I pitied our mule team. The big black mules were sweating terribly and frothing at the mouth. The sweat on their flanks shone a deep purple in the brilliant sun.

We took in 20 loads that afternoon and the only relief from the heat was the cool breeze which occasionally blew through the orchard beside the barn, and of course Sadie's homemade root beer, which little Amos brought out to us.

One of the most dramatic things connected with threshing is keeping the mules going around and around in the mow to tramp the loose straw blown in from the thresher.

64

Aaron, with a big stick, in the semi-darkness kept them going tirelessly around and around and the chaff was unbearable without a kerchief around the nose.

As the pile grew, the mules went up higher and higher and the only way to get them down was to build a kind of straw ramp up to the mow side and down.

Such a kicking and noise I never did see. One broke loose from Steffy just as he slid down, and galloped out of the barn door and broke through the corner of the garden and almost trampled little Rebecca who was playing in her wagon.

I've had several close calls with mules and horses and most every week an Amishman is trampled or injured by a horse or a husky mule. Once a mule takes off, there's no stopping him.

One time in Ben Smucker's cornfield his pair were startled by something and, with a heavy wagon, galloped a quarter mile leveling the corn, and just stopped a few feet short of an eight-foot drop to the macadam road.

The threshing was done and Amos had us in for a treat—ice cream and cookies under the grape arbor.

It was still early and the first evening star had come out when I walked up the road to my house.

MILKING
Om Melka

DURING the cold weather the only warm place besides the kitchen was milking the cows in the stable warmed by their body heat and the thick straw bedding.

It was almost dark outside and a biting March wind screeched around the barn corners as David Glick took his milking pail down from its peg in the milk house to begin the five o'clock milking.

Old Katie, David's mother-in-law and her young daughter Melinda had already finished milking the cows on one side. There were sixteen cows in all.

David has just finished this cow stable which he had designed and built himself with only the help of his brother-in-law and two brothers. After three long months working in all kinds of weather it was finally finished and now his Holsteins were housed in a nice, clean, well ventilated, whitewashed stable.

When I came in to see David I heard nothing but the hissing noise in a kind of monotonous rhythm as the milk filled the pails.

Every five minutes one of the three milkers in this half darkness would pour their pails into the strainer in the adjoining milk house.

Occasionally the little calves that David was raising would give answer to their mothers' quiet moo.

As a boy David has always liked to milk and now perhaps as it was the only time he could sit down (if only on a three-legged stool), he firmly made the milk come from the teat. His head pressed against the cow's side, I realized that this Amishman liked his cows not only because of the milk check every two weeks but they were a part of his very existence.

Just then Dolly, the big Swiss, shifted in her stall in order to reach her neighbor's hay rack and kicked over the almost full milk bucket and I heard Melinda screech a well-deserved insult in Dutch: "Donnerwedder!"

I milked the last cow and we had just finished washing out the buckets when Sarah rang the supper bell.

Washing up at the water trough, David and I wished that these bitter March winds would turn into spring breezes.

CLEANING OUT

Om Oxastall 'Raus Mischda

A RAW March wind was blowing the day I promised to help David Glick, my Amish neighbor, clean out his steer pen. David had had a big peach crop that summer and with the corn, tobacco and late potato crop he just hadn't had time to clean it out. Then too, he was planning to build his new steer pen soon.

Neither of us knew exactly where to start on this Herculean job, but as the steers would soon be rubbing their backs on the heavy stable rafters, we knew that we had to get busy. We hitched the two big horses Jack and Bill up to the manure *mischd* spreader and backed it alongside the steer pen door. What a "pitching" time we had! That morning we took out ten loads before the midday dinner bell rang. (Something of a record in Amish Olympics!)

Sarah, David's wife, knew that we had been hard at it, and had a real table "set" for us. We finished the hearty meal with some of her delicious schnitz pie and vanilla pudding. Then back to the stable. Unfortunately for the steers (but

luckily for my full stomach), a rain squall blew up and we had to finish the afternoon in the *forebay* under the overhang of the barn, sawing up boards to repair the bottom of the flat wagon.

In March all the farmers see that their planting equipment and different farm utensils are in good working order; for when the planting season begins one hasn't time to spend repairing.

The next day we finished the steer pen and put the last load of *mischd* on what would be this year's tobacco field. Just before leaving for home I saw old Mose Glick drive in the lane with his long spring wagon filled with the long wooden benches that would be needed for church at David's the following Sunday. That was another reason David had wanted his stable to be neat and clean and up to tidy Amish standards, as all his neighbors would be seeing his place next Sunday.

CHOPPING WOOD AT DAVID GLICK'S
Om Holz Hocka bei David Glick

ONE of the most necessary tasks on every Amish farm is the gathering, chopping and piling up of firewood. On the farm of my Amish neighbor David Glick, for example, wood was needed in the kettle house for heating water in the two large copper kettles, and to boil the glass jars when canning. Every Thursday a good supply was needed for Katie's red brick oven when she baked her eighty loaves; in winter wood for the stripping room stove; and every day wood must be used for the kitchen coal range where Sarah cooked and which heated the large kitchen, the only heated room in an Amishman's household.

It was young Eli's job to keep these different piles of wood replenished and neatly stacked, but first David and I had to chop and saw the wood and saw it to size.

David had thinned out his orchard this fall and we had also felled several large dead meadow trees which Mose Riehl had sawed up into four-foot chunks.

It was our job to split these pieces and chop them down to a usable size. We would first drive several triangular-shaped wedges into them with our sledge hammers till the chunks would split apart and we could do the rest with an axe. David, like his Biblical namesake, was a small man, but strong and athletic; he would take a long swing with his axe circling around his head, almost lifting him off the ground, and Whack! a perfect chop and the log would be split in two. It was pleasant working in the meadows those crisp, early fall mornings. The trees had just started to take on fall colors, although the meadow was still a soft green and luxuriant, as we hadn't yet seen an early frost. By ten we had shed our coats and were in shirtsleeves sweating in the warm Indian summer sun.

Sometimes David's little daughters, Katie and Barbie, would pull their little wagon down to where we were cutting up the wood, and they would pick up the white chips which were scattered all around us and haul them up to the house for their mother to use to start the stove. I was glad on this morning when little Katie came running down to us and shyly, in her Dutch, told us to "Komm esse." This was the weather and work that made one hungry for a good Amish dinner.

BY THE MEADOW STREAM

ON warm summer days the young Amish children from Ben Smucker's farm and R. Amos Glick's farm would come to the stream that divided the two places.

It was fun to wade about in this little swift-flowing stream. It was always cool there and the big meadow trees on either side of the stream shaded the playing children and the black and white Holstein cows that stood under their branches for protection from the hot summer sun.

The Amish farmers from the neighboring farms had built a small dam across the stream and had placed three rams which were run by the small falling streams of water and pumped water to their various barnyard watering troughs.

The children, too, would try to dam up the stream. Little Benuel standing in the middle of it would take small stones from his playmates and together they built their dam, covering the top with the red clay-like mud which they scooped

up from the stream's banks and bottom. Sometimes they were successful in stopping the water for a few minutes till the swift moving current would break through their little dam and splash the stones and mud into the water.

Occasionally a curious or thirsty cow would come to the stream, and putting her front feet into the water would stir up swirls of mud in the clear stream and send schools of guppies scurring in all directions.

After the water episodes, the children would play in the meadow, sometimes look for the skin of the August locusts which were left sticking to the bark of the meadow trees, or perhaps pick the yellow daisies in the meadow; or sometimes they would go over to Melinda's place to play on her swing which was hung from a great oak tree in the front meadow.

Today the children were excited, as Benuel's oldest brother was going to hitch up his brown and white pony to the cart and had promised to give them a ride. When he called to them from the barn, they quickly forgot the dam they were building and went scurrying across the green meadow to the waiting pony cart.

Some of our Amish friends.

COURTING

Da Henner Gayt mit da Levina

H ENRY SMUCKER and his girl   *sei maydel*   Levina Zook, David Zook's daughter, were on their way to Eli Esch's tobacco shed and the Sunday-night Sing to be held there about nine o'clock.

After Sunday morning milking, feeding and then cleaning out the stalls (only the necessary work is done by the Amish on Sunday), Henner spent two hours carefully polishing the shiny buckles on his Sunday harness and shining up the already spotless *weggele* so that when the sun hit the shining wheels, blinding highlights leapt from them. This rig was Henner's main pride in life.

His horse, Bill, was as black and lithe looking as the wagon. Ben Smucker had given Henry this horse just two months ago when at sixteen, he had joined the Church.

After the long morning church service and visiting across the field with the Huyard boys, Henry spent another hour currying and combing Big Bill to a beautiful velvety gloss.

When he picked Levina up at the end of her lane just as it was getting dark, she couldn't help exclaiming in Dutch, "My what a beautiful horse and rig." *Siss ovver 'n shainer gaul un 'n shay weggele*.

Henner had known Levina since the first grade at the Beiler School. On warm spring and fall days, Henner would ride his pony over to school and most every morning he'd meet Levina at her lane and together they'd ride on the little brown and white pony.

Tonight was an especially lively Sing. All the boys and girls were in good voice and the pie and cider were a real treat.

Henner and his friend David sat together on the long benches which had been put on the barn floor and the girls sat opposite giggling and exchanging merriments between their droll, almost gregorianlike chants.

One little Amish boy, out by the Silo, exploded a fire cracker which brought a long series of whinnies and stomping from the horses stabled below.

Buggies started to leave about eleven o'clock. Just past the meadow David tried to pass Henner and this was Henner's chance to show off Big Bill. With a sharp crack of the whip the race was on. Out onto the macadam road, ducking low to miss the willow branches and looking like two Roman charioteers, the boys drove their horses in a maddening, but well controlled dash, for almost a third of a mile. Big Bill was too much for David's horse and outdistanced him.

Levina, a little shaken by the wild ride, clutched tightly to Henner's arm as they drove down her lane.

THE AMISH WEDDING

Huchzich

IT is November, the wedding month for the Amish. One can read in the Lancaster papers under marriage applications the names of many Amish couples— Glick and Fischer, Stoltzfus and Beiler, Esch and Smucker.

By November, the last hay crop is in the barn, the corn has been husked and the potatoes are picked and bagged.

Today is Tuesday, the day set for Elam Esch and Rachel Smucker's wedding. (Amish weddings take place only on Tuesdays and Thursdays).

It is a day for all the young folks. For weeks before the wedding Rachel had been preparing for it, setting the house in order, carefully transplanting the colorful leafed coleus plants from the front garden into earthen pots to stand in straight lines in the sun porch. Just last week she finished quilting her rose pattern spread and had it tucked away in her cedar dower chest *kischt*. All week before, David, Rachel's father, and her oldest brother Emanuel had worked feverishly to finish the new chicken house in the lower meadow. Yesterday they had finished it and painted it white with the traditional green trim. In the early morning mist it looked like a little white ship to Rachel.

Today was another Indian summer day—more like spring than fall. Of course, Rachel had been up quite late with her sister Amanda, putting some last minute stitches on her wedding dress. She had chosen blue for her dress, and over this she would wear her white stiffly starched apron and kerchief for the last time, until her funeral. Married women wear black aprons and black kerchiefs.

Rachel slept later than usual this morning and was not awakened by the usual rooster crows, but rather by the smell of roasting meat, mingled with the fragrant odor of fruit pies. Her two aunts had been in the kettle house before daybreak roasting the meat in the large bake oven *bockoffa* and finishing the pies *boie* which had not been baked the evening before. The kettle house looked like a king's kitchen from the Middle Ages, with rows of chickens, geese, hams, a side of beef and dozens of pies, thickly coated, iced spice and chocolate and nut cakes. This is a feast day too!

Her bridegroom on his father's farm across the way was going about his usual morning chores. Through her window Rachel thought she saw him in the distance as he went to the barn to feed and water the stock. Young Elam was the object of many a friendly jest this morning. His younger brother Amos had knotted his shoe laces together and he had almost stumbled over himself. His two cousins from White Oak arrived late last night and he had arisen to help them stable their horses. Together the three young men had a drink of whiskey in the barn from the bottle Elam's father kept in the horse medicine box (as a kind of pre-wedding celebration).

In his newly pressed black homemade suit and stiffly starched white shirt Elam looked all the world like an early Puritan preacher, except he had a young smile and a long, bounding gait which made him look as though he was always gingerly walking in the fresh furrows guiding his plough.

Soon all the roads leading to the Smucker place resounded with the steady trotting of the well-groomed horses, and the sun was brightly reflected from the black spinning wheels. Most all of the younger folk of their church district had been invited and of course all their relatives, which made a good hundred people in all, not counting the many younger boys and girls who come with their parents and grown-up brothers and sisters.

When all was ready, Rachel and Elam went upstairs with the *Diener zum Buch,* or preachers, to receive solemn instructions on the duties of marriage.

After the service had started downstairs in the parlor (which had been made into a large room by opening the big sliding door which separated it from the kitchen) the young couple came down and took their places on two benches before Preacher Stoltzfus. There are no rings or outward signs of matrimony worn by the Amish, and after the traditional ceremony, and Preacher Stoltzfus's blessing, there followed a service like on Sunday, except for the hymns about marriage.

As soon as the young couple came out onto the porch Rachel was surrounded by all her young friends, chattering in their native dialect. Elam shook hands with all his friends and then, blushingly interrupting the women's circle, and taking Rachel by the hand, they walked into the main room to begin the wedding feast *huchzich esse* followed by their many friends. As there were not seats enough for all, the younger boys had to wait outside till the first serving was over. The visions of goose and cake and thick homemade ice cream were enough to keep them quietly subdued talking together in the front yard, or anxiously peering in at their celebrating elders.

Young Elam and Rachel were seated at one of the outer corners of the hollow square formed by the tables, surrounded by their young friends. The two fathers and older guests were at a separate table. Most of the wives and older women were busily serving the wedding guests and replenishing the bowls for the hearty appetites. When Elam nervously dropped his spoon into the gravy dish a clamor of laughter rose from his table, and Rachel, blushing too, squeezed his strong hand.

I won't mention every dish served on this wedding day, but by three o'clock even the youngest of bellies was happy and satisfied.

Elam was called out to the porch just in time to see Samuel Glick tossed not too ceremoniously over the garden fence. Samuel had been married himself only a week before and now was literally among the married men. He good naturedly straightened himself out when he was again standing, and Elam went to shake his hand, for at the next wedding he would be the one to go over the fence in the old custom.

After the evening meal, with loud cheers and good wishes the young couple ran to their shiny new buggy, with Rachel's wooden chest already in it, to start the drive to Elam's uncle's farm in the Conestoga Valley, where they would spend the next few weeks. As the sprightly horse drove down the maple-lined lane I saw Rachel's mother, Sadie, wipe a tear away and take her man's hand as we all silently watched the buggy turn into the lane and disappear behind the corn shocks.

THE YOUNG MARRIED COUPLE
Yuung Keiert Pawr

LAST November Aquila King and Mary Zook were married. I always remember that wedding feast. It was even larger than a harvest dinner.

After the meal, as is the custom, the young unmarried men tossed Aquila over the yard fence.

The young couple spent several months visiting and living with their different relatives. They went out to Mifflin County where Mary's people lived and spent several weeks over Christmas and New Year's.

The Amish do not celebrate Christmas *Grischdawg* as we do with trees and many gifts, but rather it is a simple religious holiday for them. Some close friends and relatives may exchange simple presents.

When young married couples visit around prior to settling in their own house, they will help their hosts with the various farm chores both in the kitchen and in the barn.

Come April first, Aquila and Mary were settled in the tenent farmer's house on Aquila's father's farm south of Blue Ball.

Aquila was a very quiet young man and I never got to know him well. He was a good farmer and a likeable person. Mary on the other hand was a very pretty, talkative and jovial girl. She was a good business woman and when she "stood market" on Friday and Saturday, her neatly arranged fruits and vegetables were always sold out before the close of the day.

When it came to baking *schnitz* (dried apple) *boie,* she had no equal. One supper time I had filled up on too much meat and potatoes so that when pie came around I couldn't even take a piece. She kept offering it to me and for fear of hurting her feelings I finally had to plead sick. Going out, Aquila with a broad smile, said from now on I'd best start with a piece of *schnitz boie.*

In a few years Aquila was managing his father's farm and they have moved over to the main house where Mary is tending their two little golden haired boys, Rueben and Solomon.

THE NEW BABY
s' Nei Buppli

IT was like any other spring morning on David Glick's farm except for the black auto parked beside the silo. This was an exceptional thing to see at daybreak on an Amish farm. It was Dr. Rankin's auto. Inside the farmhouse the miracle of a new life was taking place. Outside in the barn David and his hired boy Yonnie King were going about the milking, the feeding and the bedding of the animals as they did every morning.

The only sign of activity about the house was when Katie Stoltzfus, David's kindly mother-in-law, would go bustling across the porch to her wing of the house to fetch more blankets or something needed for the new life.

David and Yonnie had almost finished the milking when Old Doctor Rankin appeared at the stable door, bag in hand, and announced, "Well young man, you have a son." David told Yonnie to finish milking his cow for him and quietly accompanied the doctor into the house to see his first son. Old Jake Glick, David's father, was sitting on the rocker next to the warm kitchen stove and David's two little daughters, Melinda and Barbie, were sitting on his lap—all curious and excited over their new baby brother. Old Jake was happy; the son of his youngest son would be named Jacob too.

Sarah, the mother, had a tired but radiant smile as she raised the spread to show her husband the little head and body close beside her. David was so happy over his first son.

When the child was a few weeks older David could be seen most every night rocking little Jake to sleep in the same wooden cradle where old Jake had spent his infancy. Every day Old Jake would drive up for dinner and after Sarah had nursed her child Jake would tenderly rock his youngest grandson to sleep. Perhaps he sensed that he would not see this little one much longer, for Old Jake died before the child was a year old. Into this new life lived on some of the qualities that had made him such a gentle, kind and good man.

SHOPPING IN NEW HOLLAND
Noch Nei Holland Gay Eikawfa

LITTLE Emma was excited today. She was going to drive to New Holland with her mother and Aunt Naomi to go shopping. Already her mother had hitched up Bill to the market wagon and was helping Naomi to carry out and load the apples which they had promised to their Amish neighbor Lizzie, down at the place of R. Amos (of the Glick Amoses). Driving out of the lane of Amos's farm, Emma waved hello to young Sammy who was hoeing tobacco in the field along the road. They turned off the country dirt road onto the main white pike leading to New Holland. Little Emma liked to hear the sharp noise of the horse's hooves on the cement highway. It was a beautiful early August day. Looking out the open rear of the wagon, Emma watched the turkey buzzards soaring in circles high in the sky, and along the road were the dancing clouds of yellow butterflies. Occasionally Emma would be startled by the loud horn of a big auto which, like a wild animal, would roar around the slow moving wagon.

In New Holland they hitched up behind Robinson's cloth and clothing store. Emma took her mother's hand and together the two women and Emma entered the store and went down to the basement floor where hundreds of rolls of different materials and cloth were on display on the long tables and the shelves around this "largeroom" of the store. Emma loved to walk down the aisles looking at all the different materials, sometimes stopping to touch the bright colored stuff or rub her little fingers over the soft rolls of corduroy. Amanda and Naomi bought several yards of the wine colored cloth to make into workdresses and some bright blue cloth for Emma's father's work shirts and some gray wool material for a pair of Sunday pants for Emma's oldest brother Isaac.

Coming up from the basement Emma's mother saw a small pair of black, high-topped shoes on the bargain tables. Holding them alongside her daughter's foot they looked just right—and a good buy, too.

Emma ran down to the wagon to fetch her rabbit box. Her mother had

given her some money last week for helping to clean the eggs before boxing them, and now she was going to buy a pair of white rabbits across the street at Stauffer's hardware store.

After buying the rabbits Emma went down to the general store where the two women were buying their supplies. Emma's mother gave her the gallon can of molasses to carry down to the wagon. The Amish women only buy staples, such things as salt, lye to make homemade soap, sugar and cereals. They raise most all of the food that they need, and every winter they butcher a pig and a steer for their meat, and either have it frozen or can the meat in large two-quart jars. It's a real treat in winter to eat their homecanned fruits and vegetables.

The women finished their shopping and they started back for home. On the way back they stopped off at the old stone Mascot Mill for a bag of flour. Emma proudly held one of her rabbits out the back of the wagon for Miller Zook to see. Laughing and petting the rabbit's nose, he said, "She's pretty nearly as white as my flour" *Siss schier so weiss os mei mehl.* Emma was a happy little girl that afternoon as she carried her two new rabbits out to their pen in the cow stable.

QUILTING
Om Gwilda

LINDA spent the hour before dinner setting up the old wooden quilting frame in the parlor which was used only for company and church. Linda was Katie's only unmarried daughter although with all these visits from Levi King, Sam Zook's hired boy, it looked like she'd soon be publishing her marriage banns in this coming November.

Linda, now nineteen, had been preparing her hope chest *huf kischt* for the past six years. She now has six embroidered pillow cases *sex haigella kuppa -kissa,* dresser scarfs *dresser ticha,* towels *handticha,* and one quilt *gwild.*

Today with the help of her friends, she would finish her second large quilt. The designs were from an old pattern Linda's grandmother had used and in turn given to Linda. The big red tulips with green leaves growing out of terra-cotta pots with a diamond design around the edges was a lively and colorful contrast to the somber and plain dress of the Amish.

Sabina Glick arrived after the mid-day dinner, bringing her daughters Anna Mary and Rachel to play with Linda's nieces. Then Linda's old maiden aunt, Sadie Stoltzfus and Steffy's wife Rebecca and her sister Sarah all took places on chairs around the large stretched quilt. Laughing and chattering in Dutch, they deftly stitched the big bold pattern onto the quilt. Linda was kept busy cutting out the patterns and pressing them with her flatiron. After two hours of constant stitching, Linda served her guests some of her homemade *schpeiss kuuche* and lemonade. Her little tiger kitten almost got the cake first when she jumped up on the side table, but Linda shushed her off in time. Another hour of sewing and the quilt was completed.

Linda thanked her Amish neighbors and went to the stable to help them hitch up their horses. She promised Barbara, a year younger than herself, to come to her quilting the following week. Old Sadie stayed on to chat with Katie on the front porch.

Before supper Linda proudly folded her new quilt and carefully tucked it away in her cedar chest.

On Sunday when young Levi brought her home from the Sing, she shyly brought him over to her chest and holding the kerosene lamp, let him peep in at the beautiful bright quilt.

With a bashful smile he softly exclaimed, "My, what a nice quilt," *Oi, was for'n schainer gwild!* while placing the lamp back in its overhead holder.

94

COW SALE AT NEW HOLLAND

Kie Fendu

WHENEVER I go to the sales at the New Holland Sales Barn, the outstanding things I observe are cows, horses and beards.

The crowd is mostly Amish. Long flowing beards, gray beards, sable beards, short red and brown ones on the newly married men. And sitting opposite them, like judges in an old Biblical scene, the solid row of black, broadbrimmed hats, frock coats and beards.

Some were in groups of three or four, discussing the good and bad points of the bull just led in by one of the attendants. Others were looking at the pens for a bargain and one was shrewdly bidding, letting the auctioneer know he was doing so by scratching his ear.

I was sitting with David Zook on one of the high tiers overlooking this dramatic scene. Dave and I had been remodeling Sam Zook's steer-shed that morning. Sam was Dave's son. But we took the afternoon off to attend the cow and bull sale held every Thursday. Horse sales were held on Monday.

The bulls started to thrash around, and it took two strong boys to hold the prize bull's neck ring.

Sam King finally bought this animal for seven hundred and thirty dollars.

Next the English cattlemen with their cattle canes drove a mother and her calf into the runway between the two rows of seats. I saw Dave's eyes light up and I knew this was why he had come.

She was a good sized registered Holstein and had a well-filled-out calf.

Dave kept in the bidding and got them for three hundred and twenty dollars.

The next young bull came running out of the pen dragging his attendant with him and not until three men grabbed the nose rope, did they get him wrenched around in front of the auction stand.

This auction barn with its high-beamed ceiling, Gothic windows and tanbark runway suggested the drama of a bullfight, the action of a circus and the vastness of a cathedral.

At the main entrance a heavy-set Dutchman was selling succulent wieners and kraut and all sorts of penny candy *so schlekerwaise* to tempt the crowd.

After the sale, which was over about four o'clock, Dave and I went down to the blacksmith shop on the grounds where Dave had left his horse, Jack, to be shod.

After arranging to have his cow and calf hauled, we got in his wagon and drove back to Smoketown.

THE FARM SALE

Bauera Fendu

THE farmland in the Amish section of Lancaster County is becoming scarcer and also more expensive. So when Widow Burkholder offered her fifty-acre farm, just outside of Blueball, for sale at public auction, there were many Amish wagons to be seen among the autos parked along the pike and in the front fields leading to the farmhouse.

When Enos Burkholder, a Mennonite and owner of this good farm, had died last month, his widow had to sell the place, as their only son had left the farm and taken work in town (a thing that would rarely happen in an Amish family).

In spite of the cold gray November day there was a large crowd milling around the front porch, the wives, inspecting the varied array of furniture on the front lawn; rockers, porch settees, old four-poster beds, china, two large copper kettles; even an old spinning wheel was found in this mixed assortment. The younger folks were watching the lively corner ball game *eck balle* that was being played on a straw pile in the barnyard between some young married Amish men and some single Amish boys.

The sale had commenced at twelve o'clock and already the auctioneer *fendu growyer* had sold most all of the various farm equipment, which had been neatly arranged on the flat field between the barn and tobacco shed. There were all kinds of harrows, plows, drills, sledges and tobacco laths, lumber and several ancient-looking farm contraptions that were used long before my or even my father's time. Auctioneer Martin was in his usual good humor and between bids would make funny remarks such as guaranteeing the rockers to put you to sleep, or that the copper kettle was big enough to put your mother-in-law in. By two o'clock all of the household and farm equipment had been sold and even the corner ball game was temporarily halted as the bidding for the farm got under way.

Young Henner Lapp was especially nervous today. He and his Amish parents lived on the farm adjoining the Burkholder place. Many a time he wished he could have that place to settle on. He had married last year and had hired out to his father-in-law below Georgetown. He had worked very hard this past year and the farm had had a prosperous harvest; but he had always felt a little homesick for his birthplace and the flat rich soil of this particular region. His father Benuel had told him at market to come up this Saturday, and they could watch the sale together.

The bidding started at six hundred an acre and was up to seven-fifty when he saw his father-in-law and father quietly talking together under the pear tree a short distance from the porch steps where auctioneer Martin was vigorously taking the bids. His heart jumped for a moment when he thought that perhaps they were considering buying the place. He watched them closely for several minutes

as the bids went up to eight-fifty, eight-seventy-five, nine hundred dollars, without seeing any sign of a bid from either of them. He relaxed into a quiet unconcern until he was suddenly startled by the auctioneer's voice announcing, "Sold to Benuel Lapp at nine hundred dollars an acre." His father was a shrewd one! He had signaled his bid each time by merely scratching his ear. Together the two fathers had bought him and Rebecca this choice farm. Still bewildered, he was greeted by his father saying in his kindly tone, "Well Henner, we'll see what you can do with your own place." *Well, Henner, nu sayn mer was du mit dei eigne blotz mache konnscht.* He could hardly wait to tell Becky his wife who was "standing market" in Lancaster that afternoon. All his Amish friends crowded around him and some shook his hand. The two fathers signed the first sales papers and just before I left I saw the two old men and the young Henner having a wiener in the red brick kettle house where two farm women had been selling refreshments to the crowd. The two white-bearded men were happy that their youngsters now had their own place where they could raise a family and lead good lives.

APPLE SCHNITZING

Eppel Schnitzing

A CHATTER of Pennsylvania Dutch could be heard coming from David Glick's kettle house on this particular crisp September evening. Several Amish *weggeli* were drawn up under the *forebay* and behind the barn. Every so often, a young Amish boy or girl would come out of the kettle house carrying a box of apple parings. They would take them down to the pigpen and tilting the box on the upper fence rail would scatter them on the ground to the pigs who were hungrily awaiting this delicacy.

Inside the kettle house was an apple *schnitzing,* or paring party. Seated on chairs and apple crates around the red-bricked room were David Glick, his wife Sarah and several of their relatives. Each had a little metal box-shaped apple parer *eppelschayler.* They would pick out an apple from the basket beside them, insert it in the parer and with a quick turn of the little handle that worked the knives the red skin would be off and would drop wiggling like a snake into the paring box. Then the apples were cored and put in the large copper kettles where Katie and Sarah were slicing them up and putting them on long shallow tin trays in the bake oven which would bake the moisture out of them.

The air in the kettle house had the appetizing smell from these drying apples and not all the apples that I was *schnitzing* found their way into the oven!

While these almost mechanical movements of mass production apple paring were going on, the Amish men and women, mostly younger married couples, would keep up a steady chatter, and occasionally all would laugh when a particularly funny thing was said or done. One time David gave his wife an uncored apple to *schnitz,* and she, unaware, started to cut it up till blushingly she discovered the joke.

In order to grease the tiny crank on the apple parers David had a piece of speck (ham fat) that we passed around to rub over them. David jokingly said he was getting so hungry he thought he'd have a bite of it. This was Sarah's cue to fetch in some good brown drop cookies, and a jug of freshly pressed cider.

It was now quite dark and the younger children who had been playing in the yard and barn were sleepy, some already asleep leaning against their parents' legs or against the empty apple crates around the room.

This friendly communal group finished *schnitzing* some ten bushels of apples for David; they had only to be bagged and hung up in the attic till a delicious *schnitz* pie is wanted in the coming winter. These people have their fun and pleasure while still getting a necessary job done.

Going out the lane I saw Jonas's Naomi already fast asleep in her mother's arms. I said goodbye to David and Sarah, and walking past the pig-shed I heard the pigs still grunting, looking for a stray paring or anticipating some more.

THE SING

Singa

ON a Saturday or Sunday evening one of the young Amish boys or girls would invite young people from their own, or another district as well, to a Sing or gathering at their father's farm.

It was almost dark on this June evening when I walked up to the cornfield overlooking Ben Smucker's farm. Ben's barn looked like a stage set. Everything was centered on the bright gas lanterns that were hung from the rafters of the main barn floor. The barn doors were wide open and were flat against the barn side like the pulled-back curtains in a stage play. Two long wooden tables had been set up on the floor with the Sunday church benches on either side of them. In the half-darkness I could see the Amish boys unhitching their horses and leading them down to the stable. One group of younger boys was playing a practical joke on a comrade and was pushing his black buggy some distance into the apple orchard beside the barn. This whole scene reminded me of one of the Brueghel paintings of sixteenth-century Flemish peasants. One of the groups of young people was admiring the horse that Henner Smucker had bought at the sale last week. Most of the girls were seated on the benches on either side of the tables, chattering in Dutch and sometimes laughing at a particularly funny antic by one of the boys in front of the barn entrance. One of the younger boys had climbed up onto a barn rafter and had dropped an old dried leaf of tobacco down on the girls. While they were screaming and laughing after him, he disappeared down the other side of the hay mow.

By now some fifty wagons with their shafts sticking in the air were scattered around the barn and stable *forebay*. Henner and his sister Rachel, who were

hosts for that evening started out the singing. For a moment, hearing the monotonous, gregorian-like chants floating across the meadow, I thought I was in an old-world monastery at evening vespers. Even the tall silo beside the barn helped to give it a cathedral-like silhouette. The singing gradually brought all the boys into the barn filling the benches so that several bales of straw as well as the wooden beams on either side of hay lofts had to be used for benches. Occasionally the shrill whinney of the horses stabled below or the eerie hoot of the summer night-owls would disturb their singing.

These young Amish people take their religion and their singing seriously. For a full hour they sang their songs all in a kind of mixture of high German and their regular dialect, from their *Ausbund,* the sixteenth-century hymnal.

Not till Henner and his sister brought in two large cans of pretzels *bretzel* cakes, and several gallons of lemonade did they again resume their party and carefree mood. Young Rueben King started to play a "hoe down" piece on his mouth organ. Although dancing is frowned upon by their elders, four couples and a "caller" started up a square dance on the main floor of the steer-shed adjoining the barn.

Young Henner was glad the singing had stopped for awhile so that he had a chance to come over to the girls' side of the table and sit down with his particular girl, Levina Fischer. When the Sing started up again Henner remained sitting beside her in spite of the giggles of the girls and the winks from his friends across the table.

It was past twelve now, and they had just finished one long song when one of the mischievous young boys came running in onto the barn floor holding on to a frisky horned billygoat that he had untied from its stake in the orchard. The fierce little billy made a lunge for a group of girls and they just jumped up on the straw bales in time. All the boys were laughing and the goat let out a loud "Baaa" along with them. When the billy started to nibble the pretzels in the open can, Henner got a little vexed and gave him a sharp rap with a piece of harness that sent him running back into the orchard.

Going out the door to help his young friends lead out their horses from the stable, Henner's heart fell when he heard his cousin Eli ask Levina if he could take her home, but Levina with a half shy look in Henner's direction said she'd have to stay and help Rachel clean up and would go home with Henner.

Driving through the still countryside late that night, taking Levina down to her father's farm in White Horse, Henner got up enough courage to hold her hand and ask her to be his girl.

THE FIRE

's Feier

I HAD just finished a late supper and stepped outside to see the full harvest moon rise over Sam Zook's cornfield when the loud barking of my beagle made me look to the north fields behind our studio. What first appeared to me to be a brush fire near Sam Esch's barn *scheier* suddenly with a dull puff-like report sent flames shooting into the air seventy feet high. The whole barn was afire. With a shout to my father I was off across the lower meadow.

In front of the flaming barn I saw Sam run out of the open stable door pulling the two terrified mules to safety just as the flames engulfed the entire stable. Luckily his twenty cows were left out in the meadow that night.

By this time Ben Smucker and his boys had run up from their place.

The flames were so hot we couldn't breathe within thirty feet of the barn. We heard the fire sirens coming from the Eden fire house and immediately we dragged logs and stones down to the small stream and dammed it up for a source of water for the fire hoses.

Just before the roof of the shed alongside the barn caved in, we managed to get a heavy bull rope around the front of the big steam tractor. With desperate tugs, we pulled the tractor clear, as hot sparks and pieces of debris flew around us.

Sam already had a bad cut on his back when a timber struck him while leading the mules to safety.

The barn was past saving, but now the wind had shifted and was blowing red hot embers all over Sam's house which was only twenty yards away. We kept two fire hoses constantly drenching the porch's brick walls and roof.

Sam's wife was expecting a baby and this sudden shock put her in near hysteria.

The women folk led her to the fire chief's auto where she was able to get away from the large crowd which had been attracted by this bright light in the autumn evening's darkness.

By this time the flames had devoured the entire barn roof. We could make out the hay wagon on the barn floor as it crashed along with the falling rafters to the stables below.

Another hour and only stone walls were standing as the timbers burned vividly, lighting up the sky and orchard on the hill behind the barn.

Luckily the wind changed again and the house was out of danger, although the porch around the *kesselhus* was charred beyond repair.

I could tell by the look on Sam's strained face that he was sick. All his hay crop, thirty pigs he hadn't been able to get out, his new silo just filled with

winter silage gone with the barn. His Amish neighbors with beads of perspiration and water dripping from their faces and beards tried to console him.

The following day I went over with his neighbors and helped clean up the rubble around the still smoking barn site.

We weren't positive what had started it but most likely spontaneous combustion.

We had lost about ten barns in Lancaster County from spontaeous combustion in the hay mows that year.

With this unseasonable heat and rain most of the farmers had to risk taking

their hay in before it was completely dry or it would rot if left too long in the field.

Next day Joe Riehl, the Amish carpenter, was up at Sam's measuring up for a new barn.

Within a month we had a big raising *scheirufschlagge* and a new frame barn appeared on the original site.

All his Amish neighbors donated their time to helping him rebuild it. His father and father-in-law paid for the lumber.

What might have meant ruination for some farmers proved to be only a temporary setback for this Amishman.

SOME AMISHMEN GO ABROAD

Dayl Amische Gaina ins Old Lond

IT was still dark when Johnathan Zook and I finished giving our horses their morning oats and water. Looking out through their stalls, an unfamiliar scene greeted us. Instead of the lush green fields and woods of our Lancaster County, there was a great expanse of dark green water. We were on a cattle boat headed for Europe.

Johnathan Zook and Tommy Lapp, Amish boys and I had volunteered our services as "Sea-going Cowboys" to the Brethern Service Committee, who had donated the livestock to the UNRRA organization.

We had embarked from New York, September 10th, 1945, on the old reconverted cattle boat, the *S.S. Virginian* with about three hundred horses, all bred mares and some two hundred and fifty cows.

I was one of the youngest cowboys in this mixed group of Brethern, Mennonite, Quakers and my two Amish friends.

Most of the men were farmers from the mid-west and Pennsylvania. It was a real sacrifice for these men to leave their families and venture on this long and sometimes hazardous mission.

Johnathan and Tommy had never been ten miles from home except once when they went on a trip to western Pennsylvania to select some beef cattle for their father's farm.

They would stand for hours hanging on to a guard rail, looking across the never-ending water.

One day Johnathan asked me if there wouldn't perhaps be a bump or series of turns when we went around the earth's side.

He couldn't imagine a gradual round earth, but rather thought of it as a series of sharp turns which our ship had to navigate.

For the first few days, most of the men were sea-sick. Poor Enos Fischer never did leave his bunk for the eighteen stormswept days and lived only on crackers and lemons.

The two Amish boys and I, had asked to care for the one hundred and twenty horses quartered in the rough stalls built on the stern weather deck.

Although we weren't protected from the weather as in the three lower holds, we liked being on top deck where we could see all that was happening on the ship and on the sea.

The horses had to be kept standing the eighteen days for fear of becoming sick with cholic. We had two veterinarians who were constantly making rounds of the horses. In spite of adverse conditions, we lost only ten mares. Many died as a result of miscarriages, but we had eight calves born in the hold where the Holsteins were quartered.

Occasionally a horse would become ill or perhaps just slip on the wet planks and we would be awakened at night and try and get her up. Sometimes it took twelve strong men and many ropes to raise the sick or frightened animal.

One night I was awakened by Tommy Lapp who was on watch duty. Big eyed, he told me that while making rounds on the stern in most stalls he had seen a huge liner loom out of the thick night fog, and as our turnscrews lifted us vibrating out of the water, he had seen the liner nose past our stern.

Every morning we had a brief prayer service following the five o'clock breakfast and in the evenings, after a long day's work of tending the horses, we would gather in one of the stern mess halls and sing hymns, usually led by Jake Ebersole, one of the best liked cattlemen. Jake became ill in Stockholm on our way home and was flown to London for a stomach operation, where to the grief of all of us he died. He had many friends among this mixture of faiths, and many of us still write to and visit his widow.

Our trip took us past Ireland, northward, skirting the picturesque Scotch farms of the Orkney Islands, through the Kattegat straights, past the Danish castle of Elsinore, through the North Seat into the Baltic, and to our destination, Danzig, renamed Gdansk, by the Russian occupation troops.

As we rounded the entrance to the harbor, the Pilot skillfully guided us past the many broken and capsized ships—our first taste of war's ravages.

My Amish friends regained confidence when docking—they heard many hellos and cheers in German. (Danzig is still fifty percent German.)

When the UNRRA authorities took us to visit the Polish farms in what had been Prussia, Johnathan and Tommy were in their element. They couldn't get over the way the Polish farmers said gid-up, "Brrh". It was more of a high shrill gargle, and even today when I visit them on their farms, they still greet me with this odd sound.

I met a man who had been raised in the United States. His parents were Polish, and all his American citizenship papers had been destroyed in the war, and he was trying to secure new ones to enable him to return to the States. He took us all over the old city, meeting people and seeing things which would have been impossible on our own. When we left, we wanted to give him something in gratitude. He told us that his greatest worry was shoes to see him through the approaching winter. I gave him a pair, and in return he brought me a pair of old skiis he had used in happier times on the snow-covered hills around Danzig.

Climbing up the gangplank that night with a pair of skiis over my shoulder, brought a lot of laughs and kidding from the regular crew members.

Then on to Sweden for another ten days where we picked up a return cargo of wood pulp in North Sweden.

Coming through the North Sea one windy day, Johnathan and I were on mine watch. Many were still adrift in that area. Suddenly a huge wave rose in front of us, and aghast, we saw the ominous black metal ball hurtling towards our ship. For what seemed like eternity, we waited for the explosion, but to this day I don't know what happened to it. We rang the ship's bell and immediately afterwards reported it to the skipper who charted its probable course and radioed

it in to the nearest land station. Having coffee in the mess hall that night, Yonnie exclaimed to me in Dutch, "That was the closest call I've ever had." *Sell wawr me naiyscht.*

We stopped at Southampton to bring home two hundred war-tired G.I.'s. One night on the way home I was chosen to give a brief talk on Peace and read a scripture from the Bible. I was a bit wary of the reaction on the many G.I.'s, some still with unhealed wounds, sitting with us in the mess hall, but I was surprised that, following the talk, I acquired many friends from this group of war-hardened men who agreed with me that war was no means of settling differ-

ences among nations. I realized how true this was after seeing the aftermath of war which seemed worse than the actual waging. The stunted growth of older children, the undernourished Polish babies, many of whom had never tasted milk, the stunted growth of the older children, the hovels where people were forced to live until they could rebuild their cities, were just a part of war's horrible result.

Steaming into New York harbor three months later, (but it seemed like three years for our cattlemen) the song "Sentimental Journey," which came over the loud speaker of the U.S.O. boat that met us, hardly seemed appropriate to us, the cattlemen, or to the soldiers standing on the decks.

CHURCH
G-may

IT has been a long sermon for little Isaac as he sits straddling his father's knee. After three hours he is almost asleep and no longer listens trying to understand an occasional High German word from Preacher Stoltzfus.

Chosen by lot last year Preacher Stolzfus speaks in a shrill sing-song manner, but his words are full of truth and sincerity.

John, Isaac's father, still listening intently to the scripture reading, seeing his little son almost asleep, takes a large white handkerchief from his coat pocket and almost unconsciously twists it into a ball around his palm and knots two corners into ears to form a little white mouse.

Isaac's eyes come to life as he twists and pulls at the white cloth for another half hour.

His little sister, Rebecca, just two years old, is asleep in her mother's arms on the other side of the room where all the married women and single girls are sitting.

Outside the frosted windows the sun is reflecting brightly off the snow-covered landscape and in the stable little Isaac can just make out the horses' heads and can see their smokelike breath in the winter coldness.

The hired boy, Enos Beiler, misses church today to stay in the stable with the visiting church members' horses.

Old Mose, John's father, seeing Issac finally asleep, quietly lifts him over on his lap and with one hand holding *Das Ausbund* (Hymnal) and with the other little Isaac, bends his head in prayer. Isaac stirs slightly as the long pointed beard brushes across his cheek.

Church ends and the benches empty of these long-bearded Christians.

John stoops to pick up his handkerchief.

The men, wearing their winter capes and greatcoats, leave with their families, some driving sleighs on the snow packed roads.

FOOT WASHING

Fees Wesha

IT is the day of communion *nachtmohl*. All the Amish wagons in our district are lined up around Smucker's barn and silo. It is a shining June day.

Inside his house the bareheaded men are seated together on the long wooden benches. Across the room the women are seated, all dressed in their starched spotless aprons and prayer caps.

Preacher Riehl has just finished a fiery sermon on the Ten Commandments.

After a long prayer in German (all the service is held in German) the men and women bend down, take their shoes and stockings off and bring the buckets our from under their benches.

David Glick stands holding onto the bench with one hand as his neighbor, Eli Esch, on his knees, rubs water over both of his feet. He in turn does the same to Eli, and Ben does the same to Jacob, and Isaac to Samuel, Chris to Enos, followed by a kiss on the cheek—a simple symbolic ceremony of humility.

The women are doing the same. Amanda washes Levina's feet, Naomi washes Rachel's, Emma washes Sarah's, till they have completed the ritual.

Following this they kneel as the message of love is read from the Bible, ending their communion.

There is a simple lunch of cheese, *baluunie*, jelly and bread.

Going out they again shake their neighbor's hand.

In the bright sun, around the *weggeli*, many straw-hatted groups form, some talking about the sermon *breddich* and farming and others just visiting before hitching up for the drive home.

HOME FROM CHURCH

Daheim fun der Gmay

LITTLE Phillip clutches tightly to his mother's hand as his father Samuel Stoltzfus drives the family wagon home from church. It's a bumpy road from Leacock to their farm back of Bareville. Phillip, just eight months old is already accustomed to the sharp jolts and bouncing of the carriage. His mother Amanda hums a German lullaby and in spite of the jostling and the light spring rain that has just started to sprinkle in on them, little Phillip goes fast to sleep still holding his rattle *schpiel* made of several yarn spools on a string.

In the back of the wagon his older brothers and sisters are chattering in Dutch to one another as they peer out the one rear window at the autos going past them.

Little Amanda can't wait to get home to finish sewing her doll's apron and Sammy, fourteen, is going to hitch up his pony, Bob, to the homemade cart and take a trot over to visit his Amish friends Eli and Aaron Stoltzfus.

When they arrive home Samuel will unhitch and do the evening feeding before milking and perhaps have time to read over the passage in the Bible which preacher Mose had talked about in church today.

Amanda will nurse Phillip before getting supper and the children will go about the simple pleasures allowed them on Sundays till supper when Amanda will call them to their plain Sunday meal of tomato or cracker soup and *baluunie* sandwiches. (The Amish seldom have large Sunday dinners unless they have visitors.)

Today, on arriving home, Samuel sees the two calves loose in the corn field and together he and Sammy race to get them. Too late—they have eaten too much corn and the following day die from colic.

It seems Sammy didn't drive the nails in the locust fence gate properly and they pushed out.

Samuel is very angry of course and doesn't allow Sammy to use his pony for some time.

Sammy knows that his poor fence mending had caused his father a great loss.

The Amish funeral.

THE AMISH FUNERAL

Die Leicht

I HAD never seen so many Amish *weggeli* together on the pike as last spring when the Amish preacher Daniel Stoltzfus died. The rectangular black wagon drawn by two horses and containing the coffin led the long procession which twisted around Weaver's Hill on the way to the Amish burying ground back of Leola.

Old preacher Stoltzfus had died on Tuesday while he was quietly sitting on the sun porch of his youngest son's place. Little Naomi had thought that her Grosse Daddy was just sleeping and had playfully tried to crawl on his lap when Rachel, who was making some dresses on her sewing machine at the other end of the sun parlor, noticed that the old man's eyes were shut and life was gone. Tearfully she called her husband who was planting corn in the lower field.

Preacher Stoltzfus was well known all over Lancaster County, and in the Ohio Amish section too, for his simple, expressive, straightforward sermons. Every other Sunday for the last thirty years he had risen from the church bench to urge his Amish brethren to keep to the old ways of life, to follow the laws of Moses; and he would quote from one of the old Martyrs' stories. Watching him speak, with his large gnarled hands outstretched, and his long flowing white beard and deep resounding voice, brought to mind Abraham or some Old Testament prophet preaching to his people.

He was a practical man also. They tell the story about when too many young Amish blades began to frequent the hotel in Bird-in-hand. Preacher Dan called some of the older church members together and they solved that problem by buying the hotel and turning it into a two-family home.

Now, watching the hundreds of wagons filled with his Amish friends, children, grandchildren and great-grandchildren (there were many autos too, belonging to his "Englisha" friends), I realized the power that by its example one good life can have in the world.

At the burying ground a few simple words were said by Preacher Mose Riehl and he said the Lord's Prayer *em Herr sei gebait*. Many an Amish face was streaked with tears as, bareheaded, the coffin bearers lowered the simple pine box into the rich earth which Preacher Dan had many times cleaved with his plow, and which had given him his livelihood.

THE AMISH:
A TALK WITH DAVID
Schwetza mit David

IT was an early summer morning and I was taking my dog for a run through my Amish neighbor's meadow, when I came upon David Glick scything along the edge of the road. This was the only way he could get rid of the tall weeds that grew along this sharp embankment. With long, sure strokes which made a hissing sound he felled his crops' most deadly enemies. As I approached him a young pheasant suddenly flew up from its nest a few yards in front of us. It made both me and my dog jump and brought a good natured laugh from David. He stopped his work and reaching in his pocket drew out a honing stone *wetzschtay* and began to sharpen his scythe.

David and I often talked together about everything from the weather to politics, and whenever I had a particular question to ask about the ways or customs of the Amish David was sure to answer it for me. It seemed we were always talking together while we worked, whether it was hanging tobacco forty feet up in the peak of his barn, stripping it in the cold of winter, or cleaning out a steer stable. Sometimes Sarah, his wife, even became a bit peeved at us for fear we were slighting our work with our incessant talking.

Over the period of several years I learned much about the Amish from David. Although he didn't of course know all the historical reasons for their dress and some other customs, he knew all the religious reasons for their plain habits and so on. Here are a few of the most important facts that I have learned about the life of these simple people:

The Old Order House Amish of Lancaster County, Pennsylvania, is the strictest and most uncompromising group of the many "plain sects" living in America. These people, for the most part are farmers, live in the rural communities of America, and although only a small number actually resides in Pennsylvania, the settlement in Lancaster is the oldest and richest. The rest, including the largest settlement, in Ohio, live in other sections of the United States.

The Amish are a branch of the Plain People known as Mennonites, originally the Swiss Brethren or Anabaptists, a radical end of the Protestant Reformation in Canton Zuerich, Switzerland. The Mennonites that came to America in the early seventeen hundreds for religious and economic reasons came mostly from Switzerland and the Rhineland of Germany known as the Pfalz or Palatinate.

In c. 1693 Jacob Ammon, a Mennonite, broke away from his sect because he believed in a complete shunning; that is, if a man broke one of the tenets of the church he was to be denied any social intercourse whatsoever with any other member of the church. Ammon's followers became known as Ammon's Men, which name has since been contracted to Amishmen.

The Amish look to the Bible for their principles of daily life; they take no oaths, have no dealings with civil courts except when absolutely necessary, and Jesus' words, "Love your enemies," have developed into their main reason for non-resistance or pacifism. They use the Luther translation of the Bible, the Ausbund or hymnal, and read the old stirring stories from the Martyrs' Book. Their church services are held every other Sunday in their farm houses, as they do not believe in having church buildings. Today on the home and farm they still speak Pennsylvania Dutch, a Pfaelzer or Palatinate dialect of German. Many of the young children speak little or no English until they start school, where of course they learn it.

Like their Swiss Brethern ancestors and the Quakers, they believe in simplicity of dress. Except for their hats and shoes, all their clothing is homemade. Their plain Sunday suits, as well as their caped overcoats, are always black, trousers are sometimes dark gray although the men's work shirts and women's work dresses are often made of brilliantly colored material. The women always wear a small white organdy cap (prayer cap), black bonnets and capes, and the men wear large broadbrimmed hats. Today, even among the Amish living in different counties and states there are differences in the cut and style of the bonnets and hats. The use of hooks and eyes instead of buttons may have been a protest against the large metal buttons on the uniforms worn by the soldiers in their old home-land. Usually an Amish boy joins the church in his late teens but does not raise a beard, which is the invariable custom, until he takes a wife, and then the beard is required. The beard habit originated in Switzerland, although mustaches are forbidden, perhaps a protest against the long flowing mustaches of the old cavaliers. The women wear no makeup of any kind, do not cut their hair, but wear it braided in a roll on the back of the head. The menfolk have long hair too, cutting it in a straight line around the neck. People make the old joke about a bowl being put over a young Amish lad's head in order to make the "Dutch Boy" haircut even. The children wear the same-style clothing as their elders, although sometimes a pair of hand-me-down pants from an older brother is often a little too baggy. Young girls start wearing prayer caps when they are of an age to be considered young ladies, and all the women and girls keep their heads covered while working outdoors with kerchiefs tied in the back of the neck.

The Amish "do unto others as you would have them do unto you." They buy no regular insurance from companies; instead, they have their own communal form of insurance whereby an unfortunate member who should lose his barn or other buildings through fire or other disaster would not be ruined; and when Jonas Stoltzfus, for example, was trampled by a runaway mule at the height of harvest and had to be hospitalized, all his Amish neighbors in the Snake Hill Valley harvested his crops for him; put away his tobacco; cut the corn and filled his silo with it. There is seldom an exchange of money, but rather their labor is

traded back and forth. When Steffy Glick needed help in his first June hay harvest, David Glick and I went down to his place and worked for two long hot days raking up the hay and filling his two hay lofts. Then the following week Steffy and his hired boy came to Davy's to help with his first hay crop.

The Amish don't believe in speculation, and if, for example, one of the members is buying and selling corn or steers faster than usual he is soon advised about stopping by the bishop or the three members who are the overseers of his particular district.

The settlements are usually about thirty families to a church district, that number being about as many as can assemble in one farmhouse for the fortnightly church. The bishop, two ministers *Deiner tsum Buch* and a deacon are all chosen by lot, having been first nominated by the menfolk of the congregation. All the personal matters are brought up in church. When I visit with them at church, I go outside with the younger children and single folk while these matters are discussed. In serious cases an offender is sometimes "meided" (shunned) by the group, even by his own family, until he repents or decides to leave the church. Although this rarely happens, I know of one case where a young Amishman bought a car and kept it in an "English" neighbor's garage. He was found out and was "meided" until he sold the car and came back to his Amish ways.

The Amish travel. Many visit back and forth between the large Amish communities in Ohio, Illinois and Indiana. Recently some families moved to Maryland and Virginia from Lancaster County as the land in the latter became scarcer. There are also some as far west as Iowa and Nebraska and even farther away in some other places. Many a young Lancaster County Amishman has found his wife in western Pennsylvania, Ohio or other more distant settlements. In fact one of my Amish relatives from Adams County, Indiana, married the sister of my carpenter friend David Zook.

In Sarasota, Florida, there is a large winter settlement of "plain people" from all over the United States. Some of the older Amish folk go there in winter for their health, but the church bishops frown upon the younger people going there. Many of these younger Amish people start to "dress around," wearing T-shirts and other "gay" clothing in this hot climate and vacation atmosphere.

The Old Order House Amish have no modern conveniences such as electricity, up-to-date plumbing systems, central heating, cars, tractors or any other self-operating farm equipment, although they may have gasoline engines to run such necessary machines as milk coolers and pumps. They do not consider the modern automobile a "work of the devil," as is sometimes said in over-dramatic articles on these people, but rather they sensibly realize that if their children are to remain farmers they must not be exposed to the modern city life of radios, television and moving pictures, which are so easily accessible when one owns a car. Although their farm work is longer and harder with only horse-drawn equipment, their large families share the work and there is no time for idleness.

When an Amish farmer retires he does not sell his farm and move into a city, but he and his wife move into a separate wing of the farmhouse, which has been handed over to the youngest son, or perhaps build a separate house there, known as the "gross-dawdi haus" (grandaddy house). Usually by this time the

youngest son is married and is renting or buying the home farm from his father. The old man will pass his old age watching his grandchildren grow up and helping advise his son in the management of the farm. The money that is gained from the land is always put back into improving the farm, a fact that accounts for the Amish having the best farms and farm buildings in the nation. Should an Amishman accumulate considerable wealth he will buy another farm or farms for his sons or sons-in-law.

A divorce is an unknown thing among the Amish, although a widow or widower may remarry. A wife is loved and respected by her husband and children. The work she does is a very necessary part of their agricultural existence, and she has an enormous capacity for work. I have often wondered how an Amish mother can cook, can all the food for the winter months, make most all the clothing for her family, keep a neat yard and vegetable garden, "stand market" and even help in the fields during harvest time.

The Amish farmer's most steady source of income is from his cows. Most every Amishman keeps from ten to twenty milking cows and some buy steers to fatten over the winter or raise young heifers to sell. Some keep as many as five hundred chickens and sell their eggs to wholesalers and at the market. Wheat is also a "cash crop," as well as potatoes, tomatoes and tobacco. Tobacco is the main "cash crop" in Lancaster County. Although a considerable amount is realized from the sale of this valuable product the Amish farmer is hardly repaid for all the care, time and work he has taken in raising it. Many a farmer's crop has been entirely ruined by a late summer hailstorm.

The usual crops of hay and corn are used for feeding the stock, chickens, etc., over the winter, and very seldom is there an excess of these two feeding crops. Although the Amish still use the old-fashioned horse, as required by their religion, they practice soil conservation, rotation of crops (first adopted by their Swiss Brethren ancestors), and continually revitalize their land with manure and chemical fertilizers, a fact that has helped make Lancaster County the most productive, non-irrigated county in America. I remember a tractor salesman talking to Ben Smucker about the merits of modern tractors over horses and mules, saying that gas was cheaper than feed, etc.; but Ben, winking at me said, "Perhaps, but then your tractors don't give any manure!"

Most every Amish farm has at least one small apple or peach orchard. Sheep are raised for their wool and pigs, turkeys, chickens and ducks are also raised and are added sources of income. The women make money from the sale of their surplus garden vegetables and fruits, their canned jellies and pickles, dairy and baked products, at the large Lancaster Farmers Markets.

Although an Amish farmer will never become rich in the modern sense, he will always have a full larder, a cellar full of good, home-canned food for the winter, and as long as the seasons follow each other through the year, his family will never know want or hunger.

Among themselves the Amish are a friendly and good-natured people, and like their Swiss and Rhinelander forefathers they are always ready for a friendly joke or merriment; but naturally because of the language and religious differences it is difficult for an "outsider" to become well acquainted with them. To an "outsider" their way of life may look rather drab and difficult as they have no interest in worldly pleasures, or in any of the arts except singing and handicrafts, but they have their simple pleasures: an apple-paring bee; a quilting party; a farm or animal sale; a friendly game of corner ball; a Sunday night Sing, or just a gathering of the *Freindschoft*.